Edward Bulwer Lytton

The odes and epodes of Horace

A metrical translation into English with introduction and commentaries by Lord

Lytton

Edward Bulwer Lytton

The odes and epodes of Horace
A metrical translation into English with introduction and commentaries by Lord Lytton

ISBN/EAN: 9783742801838

Manufactured in Europe, USA, Canada, Australia, Japa

Cover: Foto ©Andreas Hilbeck / pixelio.de

Manufactured and distributed by brebook publishing software (www.brebook.com)

Edward Bulwer Lytton

The odes and epodes of Horace

EACH VOLUME SOLD SEPARATELY.

COLLECTION
OF
BRITISH AUTHORS
TAUCHNITZ EDITION.

VOL. 1057.

THE ODES AND EPODES OF HORACE
BY
LORD LYTTON.

IN TWO VOLUMES. — VOL. 2.

LEIPZIG: BERNHARD TAUCHNITZ.

PARIS: C. REINWALD, 15, RUE DES SAINTS PÈRES.

*This Collection
is published with copyright for Continental circulation, but all*

TAUCHNITZ EDITION.
Each volume 1½ Thlr.

ADAMS: Sacred Allegories 1 v.
ELLAR: Home Influence 2 v. The ompense 2 v.
a 1 v. Carr of Carrlyon 2 v. The

ITH: Windsor Castle 1 v. Saint Jack Sheppard (w. portr.) 1 v. Ire Witches 2 v. The Star-Chamber Flitch of Bacon 1 v. The Spendervyn Clitheroe 2 v. Ovingdean The Constable of the Tower 1 v. yor of London 2 v. Cardinal Pole 1w 2 v. The Spanish Match 2 v. e de Bourbon 2 v. Old Court 2 v. omfret 2 v. South-Sea Bubble 2 v. os 2 v.

R GREED," AUTHOR OF: All for ove the Avenger 2 v.
TEN: Sense and Sensibility 1 v. rk 1 v.
LATKA 1 v.
. BAYNES: Lyra Anglicana 1 v.
BELL: Jane Eyre 2 v. Shirley 2 v. The Professor 1 v.
ELL: Wuthering Heights, and 2 v.
LESSINGTON: Meredith 1 v. v. Memoirs of a Femme de . Marmaduke Herbert 2 v. Coun- (w. portr.) 2 v.
N: Lady Audley's Secret 2 v. d 2 v. Eleanor's Victory 2 v. John Legacy 2 v. Henry Dunbar 2 v. le 2 v. Only a Clod 2 v. Sir Jasper's Lady's Mile 2 v. Rupert Godwin s Fruit 2 v. Run to Earth 2 v. The Silver Cord 3 v. Sooner or

Rab and his Friends 1 v.
OWN'S School Days 1 v.
(LORD LYTTON): Pelham (w. ugene Aram 1 v. Paul Clifford 1 v. Pompeii 1 v. The Disowned 1 v. avers 1 v. Alice 1 v. Eva, and the he Rhine 1 v. Devereux 1 v. Godolkland 1 v. Rienzi 1 v. Night and The Last of the Barons 2 v. Athens f Schiller 1 v. Lucretia 1 v. Harold thur 2 v. The New Timon; Saint v. The Caxtons 2 v. My Novel ill he do with it? 4 v. Dramatic , Strange Story 2 v. Caxtoniana 2 v. iles of Miletus 1 v. Miscellaneous 1 v. Odes & Epodes of Horace 2 v.

"THE LAST OF THE CAVALIERS," AUTHOR OF: The Last of the Cavaliers 2 v. The Gain of a Loss 2 v.
"SCHÖNBERG-COTTA FAMILY," AUTHOR OF: Schönberg-Cotta Family 2 v. The Draytons 2 v. On Both Sides of the Sea 2 v. Winifred Bertram 1 v. Diary of Mrs. Kitty Trevylyan 1 v.
S. T. COLERIDGE: The Poems 1 v.
WILKIE COLLINS: After Dark 1 v. Hide and Seek 2 v. A Plot in Private Life 1 v. The Dead Secret 2 v. The Woman in White 2 v. Basil 1 v. No Name 3 v. Antonina 2 v. Armadale 3 v. The Moonstone 2 v.
"COMETH UP AS A FLOWER," AUTHOR OF: Cometh up as a Flower 1 v. Not wisely, but too well 2 v.
FENIMORE COOPER: The Spy (w. portr.) 1 v. The Two Admirals 1 v. Jack O'Lantern 1 v.
THE TWO COSMOS 1 v.
MISS CRAIK: Lost and Won 1 v. Faith Unwin's Ordeal 1 v. Leslie Tyrrell 1 v. Winifred's Wooing and other Tales 1 v. Mildrod 1 v.
MISS CUMMINS: Lamplighter 1 v. Mabel Vaughan 1 v. El Fureidis 1 v. Haunted Hearts 1 v.
DE-FOE: Robinson Crusoe 1 v.
CHARLES DICKENS: The Pickwick Club (w. portr.) 2 v. American Notes 1 v. Oliver Twist 1 v. Nicholas Nickleby 2 v. Sketches 1 v. Martin Chuzzlewit 2 v. A Christmas Carol; the Chimes; the Cricket 1 v. Master Humphrey's Clock 3 v. Pictures from Italy 1 v. The Battle of Life; the Haunted Man 1 v. Dombey and Son 3 v. Copperfield 3 v. Bleak House 4 v. A Child's History of England (2 v. 8° 27 Ngr.). Hard Times 1 v. Little Dorrit 4 v. A Tale of two Cities 2 v. Hunted Down; the Uncommercial Traveller 1 v. Great Expectations 2 v. Christmas Stories 1 v. Our Mutual Friend 4 v. Somebody's Luggage; Mrs. Lirriper's Lodgings; Mrs. Lirriper's Legacy 1 v. Doctor Marigold's Prescriptions; Mugby Junction 1 v. No Thoroughfare 1 v.
B. DISRAELI: Coningsby 1 v. Sybil 1 v. Contarini Fleming (w. portr.) 1 v. Alroy 1 v. Tancred 2 v. Venetia 2 v. Vivian Grey 2 v. Henrietta Temple 1 v.
DIXON: Lord Bacon 1 v. The Holy Land 2 v. New America 2 v. Spiritual Wives 2 v. Her Majesty's Tower 1 v.
MISS A. B. EDWARDS: Barbara's History 2 v. Miss Carew 2 v. Hand and Glove 1 v. Half a Million of Money 2 v.
MRS. EDWARDS: Archie Lovell 2 v. Steven Lawrence 2 v.
ELIOT: Scenes of Clerical Life 2 v. Adam Bede 2 v. The Mill on the Floss 2 v. Silas Marner 1 v. Romola 2 v. Felix Holt 2 v.

COLLECTION
OF
BRITISH AUTHORS

TAUCHNITZ EDITION.

VOL. 1057.

THE ODES AND EPODES OF HORACE
BY
LORD LYTTON.

IN TWO VOLUMES.
VOL. II.

THE
ODES AND EPODES
OF
HORACE

A METRICAL TRANSLATION
INTO ENGLISH

WITH INTRODUCTION AND COMMENTARIES

BY
LORD LYTTON.

COPYRIGHT EDITION.

IN TWO VOLUMES. — VOL. II.

With Latin Text.

LEIPZIG
BERNHARD TAUCHNITZ
1869.

CONTENTS

OF VOLUME II.

THE ODES.

BOOK III. (CONTINUED.)

Ode		Page
V.	The Soldier forfeits his Country who surrenders himself to the Enemy in Battle,	3
VI.	On the Social Corruption of the Time,	12
VII.	To Asteria,	18
VIII.	To Mæcenas, on the Anniversary of Horace's Escape from the Falling Tree,	22
IX.	The Reconciliation,	26
X.	To Lyce,	30
XI.	To the Lyre,	34
XII.	Neobule's Soliloquy,	40
XIII.	To the Bandusian Fountain,	42
XIV.	On the Anticipated Return of Augustus from the Cantabrian War,	46
XV.	On an old Woman affecting Youth,	50
XVI.	Gold the Corruptor,	52
XVII.	To L. Ælius Lamia,	58
XVIII.	To Faunus,	62
XIX.	To Telephus.—In Honour of Murena's Installation in the College of Augurs,	66
XX.	(Omitted.)	
XXI.	To my Cask,	72
XXII.	Votive Inscription to Diana,	76
XXIII.	To Phidyle,	78
XXIV.	On the Money-seeking Tendencies of the Age,	82
XXV.	Hymn to Bacchus,	90
XXVI.	To Venus,	94
XXVII.	To Galatea undertaking a Journey,	96
XXVIII.	On the Feast-Day of Neptune,	104
XXIX.	Invitation to Mæcenas,	106
XXX.	Prediction of his own Future Time,	114

THE SECULAR HYMN, — 118

BOOK IV.

Ode		Page
I.	To Venus,	132
II.	To Iulus Antonius,	138
III.	To Melpomene,	146
IV.	In Praise of Drusus and the Race of the Neros,	150
V.	To Augustus, that he would hasten his Return to Rome,	160
VI.	To Apollo,	166
VII.	To Torquatus,	172
VIII.	To Censorinus,	176
IX.	To Lollius,	182
X.	(Omitted.)	
XI.	To Phyllis,	190
XII.	Invitation to Virgil,	196
XIII.	To Lyce, a Faded Beauty,	202
XIV.	To Augustus, after the Victories of Tiberius,	206
XV.	To Augustus on the Restoration of Peace,	212

THE EPODES.

INTRODUCTION, ... 218

Epode		
I.	To Mæcenas,	220
II.	Alfius.—The Charms of Rural Life,	224
III.	To Mæcenas in Execration of Garlic,	232
IV.	Against an Upstart,	236
V.	On the Witch Canidia,	240
VI.	Against Cassius,	252
VII.	To the Romans,	254
VIII	(Omitted.)	
IX.	To Mæcenas,	256
X.	On Mævius setting out on a Voyage,	262
XI. and XII.	(Omitted.)	
XIII.	To Friends,	266
XIV.	To Mæcenas in Excuse for Indolence in Completing the Verses he had Promised,	270
XV.	To Neæra,	272
XVI.	To the Roman People (or Rather to his own Political Friends),	276
XVII.	To Canidia—in Apology,	284
	Canidia's Reply	290

THE ODES.

BOOK III.

(CONTINUED.)

ODE V.

THE SOLDIER FORFEITS HIS COUNTRY WHO SURRENDERS HIMSELF TO THE ENEMY IN BATTLE.

In this ode the political object of Horace is to stigmatise the Roman soldiers, who, being made prisoners—or, to use an appropriate French word, *détenus* —after the defeat of Crassus, had accustomed themselves to the country in which they were detained, married into barbarian families, and accepted military service under the conqueror; and in thus energetically representing the moral disgrace of these men, Horace is very evidently opposing some proposition then afloat for demanding their restoration from the Parthians. Such demand, which would no doubt be urged by the relatives of the *détenus*, and perhaps by many old fellow-soldiers in the Roman army, might easily have acquired the importance of what we call a party question. And if Horace here opposes it, it is pretty certain that Augustus opposed it also at that time. Hence the ode would have been written before Augustus redemanded (A.U.C. 731) the Roman captives and standards from Phraates. And the date A.U.C. 728 or

729, assigned to the ode by Orelli, is probably the true one. A demand which circumstances rendered reasonable and politic in 731, might have been very inopportune and unwise two or three years before. In aiming at his political object, Horace skilfully eludes its exact definition. He begins by saying, that as it is by his thunder we believe in Jove, so the power of Augustus will be recognised when he shall have added the Britons and Parthians to his empire. Thus, agreeably with the oratorical character of his poetry, on which I have observed in the preliminary essay, his exordium

'Tis by his thunder we believe Jove reigns
In heaven: on earth,* as a presiding god,
    When to his realm annexed
        Briton and Persian,† Cæsar shall be held!

What! hath the soldier who with Crassus served,
Lived the vile spouse of a barbarian wife?
    Shame to Rome's Senate!§ shame
        On manners that invert the Rome of old.

Marsian, Apulian, sons-in-law to foes
Of their own sires! grown grey in hireling mail
    Beneath a Median king!
        Oblivious of the sacred shields of Mars,

---

* "'Præsens divus' is obviously 'præsens in terris,' as opposed to 'cælo.'"—MACLEANE.
† Persian for Parthian, as Lib. I. Od. II. 22.

exordium propitiates the ear of the party he is about to oppose—viz., those clamorous for the restoration of the Parthian prisoners. He follows this exordium with a rapid outburst on the ignominy of these very prisoners, and then, with admirable boldness, places the argument against their restoration in the mouth of the national hero Regulus. It is in these and similar passages that Horace not only soars immeasurably above the level of didactic poetry properly so called, but justifies his claim to a far higher rank even in lyrical poetry than many of his modern critics are disposed to accord to him. He attains to that region of the sublime which belongs to heroic sentiment, and which is the rarest variety of the sublime even in the tragic drama.

CARM. V.

Cælo tonantem credidimus Jovem
Regnare: præsens divus* habebitur
    Augustus, adjectis Britannis
        Imperio gravibusque Persis.†

Milesne Crassi conjuge barbara
Turpis maritus vixit? et hostium—
    Pro Curia inversique mores!§—
        Consenuit socerorum in armis,

---

§ "Pro Curia" &c.—viz., "Shame to the Senate for the scandal to its dignity in having so long endured a disgrace so ignominious."—ORELLI.

Oblivious both of toga and of name,
And Vesta's unextinguishable fire,*
   While yet live Jove and Rome! †
      Ah! this the provident mind of Regulus

Foresaw, when arguing that to buy from Death
Captives unworthy pity, on vile terms,
   Would serve in after days,
      As the sure precedent of doom to Rome.

"I," thus he said, "have with these eyes beheld
The Roman standards nailed to Punic shrines;
   From Roman soldiers seen
      The bloodless weapons wrenched without a blow;

"Seen the stout arms of Roman citizens
Twisted, all slave-like, behind free-born backs,
   While foes retilled safe fields,
      And left expanded portals sentryless.

"Think ye, forsooth, the soldier whom your gold
Ransoms from bonds, comes back a braver man!
   No, you in this but swell
      By a fresh damage,§ the account of shame.

"Never the wool drugged by the sea-weed's dye
Regains the colours lost; never, once fled,
   True valour cares to find
      In the degenerate heart its former place.

---

  * "Horace collects the most distinguished objects of a Roman's reverence—his name, his citizenship (toga), the shield of Mars only to be lost, and the fire of Vesta only to be extinguished, when Rome should perish."—MACLEANE.
  † "Incolumi Jove." "Salvo Capitolio," Schol.—viz., the Capitol in which stood the temple of Capitoline Jove.

Sub rege Medo, Marsus et Apulus,
Anciliorum et nominis et togæ
  Oblitus, æternæque Vestæ,*
    Incolumi Jove et urbe Roma? †

Hoc caverat mens provida Reguli
Dissentientis conditionibus
  Fœdis, et exemplo trahentis
    Perniciem veniens in ævum,

Si non periret immiserabilis
Captiva pubes. 'Signa ego Punicis
  Adfixa delubris et arma
    Militibus sine cæde,' dixit,

'Derepta vidi; vidi ego civium
Retorta tergo brachia libero,
  Portasque non clausas, et arva
    Marte coli populata nostro.

Auro repensus scilicet acrior
Miles redibit! Flagitio additis
  Damnum.§ Neque amissos colores
    Lana refert medicata fuco,

Nec vera virtus, cum semel excidit,
Curat reponi deterioribus.
  Si pugnat extricata densis
    Cerva plagis, erit ille fortis,

---

§ "Flagitio additis Damnum." Orelli, Dillenburger, and Macleane agree in considering that "damnum" does not refer, as some suppose, to the loss of the ransom, but to the damage done by the example of ransoming captives who had evinced so little courage.

"If, when set free from toils, the dove will fight,
He will be brave, *He* trample Carthage down
   In some new battle-field,
      Who hath confided his own recreant self

"To faithless foes,—felt passive on his wrists
The gall of thongs, and known the fear of death;
   Mingling his country's war
      With terms of peace for his own recreant self;

"Not even conscious of the only way
By which in battle soldiers guard their lives.*
   O shame! great Carthage hail,
      Throned on the ruins of a Rome disgraced!"

Then, it is said, he turned from the embrace
Of his chaste wife and children, as a man
   Of social rites bereft,†
      A citizen no more, and bent to earth

In stern humility his manly face,
Till his inflexible persistence fixed
   The Senate's wavering will;
      And forth, bewept, the glorious exile passed.

Albeit he knew what the barbarian skill
Of the tormentor for himself prepared,
   He motioned from his path
      The opposing kindred, the retarding crowd,

---

* "Hic, unde vitam sumeret inscius,
      Pacem duello miscuit."
That is, such a man, not comprehending that it is only by his own

BOOK III.—ODE V.

Qui perfidis se credidit hostibus;
Et Marte Pœnos proteret altero,
  Qui lora restrictis lacertis
    Sensit iners, timuitque mortem.

Hic, unde vitam sumeret inscius,
Pacem duello miscuit.* O pudor!
  O magna Carthago, probrosis
    Altior Italiæ ruinis!'

Fertur pudicæ conjugis osculum,
Parvosque natos, ut capitis minor,†
  Ab se removisse, et virilem
    Torvus humi posuisse voltum:

Donec labantes consilio patres
Firmaret auctor nunquam alias dato,
  Interque mærentes amicos
    Egregius properaret exsul.

Atqui sciebat quæ sibi barbarus
Tortor pararet; non aliter tamen
  Dimovit obstantes propinquos,
    Et populum reditus morantem,

---

unyielding valour that he should save his life, confounds peace and war by making peace for himself on the field of battle. Conditions of peace belong to the state, not to the individual soldier, upon whom the state imposes the duty to fight at any hazard of life.— See Orelli's note.

† "Capitis minor." The expression signifies the man who has lost his civil rights, as did the Roman citizen taken prisoner by the enemy.

Calmly as if, some client's tedious suit
Closed by his judgment,* to Venafrian plains
  Or mild Tarentum, built
    By antique Spartans, went his pleasant way.

* The patrons were accustomed to settle the dispute between their clients.

BOOK III.—ODE V.

Quam si clientum longa negotia
Dijudicata lite relinqueret,*
   Tendens Venafranos in agros,
    Aut Lacedæmonium Tarentum.

ODE VI.

ON THE SOCIAL CORRUPTION OF THE TIME.

Macleane observes that, "As the former (five) odes are addressed more to qualities of young men, this refers more especially to the vices of young women, and so Horace discharges the promise with which this series of odes begins." To me, on the contrary, it is precisely because of the lines which so freely describe the vices of young women, single and married, that I hesitate to class this ode among those to which the introductory verse of the first ode applies. Let any man consider if a poet, as the Muse's priest, could have addressed, in the original, lines from 21 to 32, not

Roman, the sins thy fathers have committed,
From thee, though guiltless, shall exact atonement,
   Till tottering fanes* and temples be restored,
      And smoke-grimed† statues of neglected gods.

Thou rul'st by being to the gods subjected,
To this each deed's conception and completion
   Refer; full many an ill the gods contemned
      Have showered upon this sorrowing Italy.

---

* The restoration of the temples and fanes decayed by time, or burned down in the civil wars, was among the chief reforms of Augustus.—Suet., Oct. xxx.

not to freed-women and singing-girls, but to the well-born maidens and brides of Rome. That the poem was written about the same time as the others is a reasonable conjecture, and probably with the same intention of assisting the reforms of Augustus, among which Horace subsequently celebrates the stricter laws regulating and affecting marriage. But I do not think the poem was or could be one of those specially addressed to the young; and, independently of the lines I have referred to, the concluding stanza, in fierce condemnation of themselves and their immediate parents, would be very unlike the skilful way in which Horace "admissus circum præcordia ludit."

Carm. VI.

Delicta majorum immeritus lues,
Romane, donec templa* refeceris,
 Ædesque labentes deorum, et
  Fœda nigro simulacra fumo.†

Dis te minorem quod geris, imperas:
Hinc omne principium, huc refer exitum.
 Di multa neglecti dederunt
  Hesperiæ mala luctuosæ.

---

† "Smoke-grimed,"—partly by conflagrations commemorated by Tacitus and Suetonius, partly by the fumes from the sacrifices. Stated times for the washing of the statues, with solemn rites, were appointed.

Twice have Monæses* and the Parthian riders
Of Pacorus crushed our evil-omened onslaught,
   And to their puny torques smiled to add
     The spoils of armour stripped from Roman breasts.

Dacian and Æthiopian,** dread-inspiring—
One with his archers, with his fleets the other—
   Well-nigh destroyed this very Rome herself,
     While all her thought was on her own fierce brawls.

This age, crime-bearing, first polluted wedlock,
Hence race adulterate, and hence homes dishallowed;†
   And from this fountain flowed a poisoned stream,
     Pest-spreading through the people and the land.

The ripening virgin, blushless, learns delighted
Ionic dances; in the art of wantons
   Studiously fashioned; even in the bud,
     Tingles, within her, meditated sin.§

---

* Pacorus, son of the Parthian king Arsaces XIV., defeated Decidius Saxa, legate to M. Antony. Four years later, when Pacorus was dead, the Parthians defeated Antony commanding in person. It is not known who is meant by Monæses. Plutarch mentions a Parthian of that name who fled to Antony, but it nowhere appears that he bore arms against the Romans. Orelli and Macleane favour the conjecture that by Monæses is meant Surenas, who defeated Crassus, A.U.C. 701—supposing Surenas to be merely an Oriental title of dignity, and Monæses to have been the proper name of Crassus's conqueror.

** This is an allusion to the threats of Antony and Cleopatra against Rome—
      "Dum Capitolio
    Regina dementes ruinas,
     Funus et imperio parabat."
         —Lib. I. Od. xxxvii.
The Dacian archers were auxiliaries in Antony's army at Actium.

BOOK III.—ODE VI.

Jam bis Monæses* et Pacori manus
Non auspicatos contudit impetus
　Nostros, et adjecisse prædam
　　Torquibus exiguis renidet.

Pæne occupatam seditionibus
Delevit Urbem Dacus et Æthiops;**
　Hic classe formidatus, ille
　　Missilibus melior sagittis.

Fecunda culpæ sæcula nuptias
Primum inquinavere, et genus, et domos;†
　Hoc fonte derivata clades
　　In patriam populumque fluxit.

Motus doceri gaudet Ionicos
Matura virgo, et fingitur artibus;
　Jam nunc et incestos amores
　　De tenero meditatur ungui;§

By the Æthiopians is meant the Egyptian fleet. The ode must therefore have been written after the battle of Actium.

† Here Horace, tracing the corruption of the times to the contempt of the marriage-tie, whether by adultery or the excess to which the licence of divorce was carried, aids Augustus in the reforms he effected in the law of marriage.

§ "Jam nunc et incestos amores
　　De tenero meditatur ungui."

I have adhered to the received and simplest interpretation of "de tenero ungui," "from earliest youth or tender years." But another interpretation, which Orelli considers very ingenious and appears to approve, will be found in his note to the passage, "penitus ex intimis nervis"—as we say in English, "tingling to the finger-ends;" or, as the French say, clever or wicked, "au bout des ongles."

Later, a wife—her consort in his cups,
She courts some younger gallant, whom, no matter,
   Snatching the moment from the board to slip,
     And hide the lover from the tell-tale lights.*

Prompt at the beck (her venal spouse conniving)
Of some man-milliner† or rude sea-captain
   Of trade-ship fresh from marts of pilfered Spain,
     Buying full dearly the disgrace she sells.

Not from such parents sprang that race undaunted,
Who reddened ocean with the gore of Carthage,
   Beat down stout Pyrrhus, great Antiochus,
     And broke the might of direful Hannibal.

That manly race was born of warriors rustic,
Tutored to cleave with Sabine spades the furrow,
   And, at some rigid mother's bluff command,
     Shouldering the logs their lusty right hands hewed,

What time the sun reversed the mountain shadows,
And from the yoke released the wearied oxen,
   As his own chariot slowly passed away,
     Leaving on earth the friendly hour of rest.

What does time dwarf not and deform, corrupting!
Our father's age ignobler than our grandsires'
   Bore us yet more depraved; and we in turn
     Shall leave a race more vicious than ourselves.

---

* "Impermissa raptim
Gaudia, luminibus remotis."

"Raptim non est 'furtim' sed 'celeriter,' ita est statim post venerem in triclinium redeat," &c.—ORELLI.

BOOK III.—ODE VI.

Mox juniores quærit adulteros
Inter mariti vina; neque eligit,
    Cui donet impermissa raptim
        Gaudia, luminibus remotis;*

Sed jussa coram non sine conscio
Surgit marito, seu vocat institor,†
    Seu navis Hispanæ magister,
        Dedecorum pretiosus emptor.

Non his juventus orta parentibus
Infecit æquor sanguine Punico,
    Pyrrhumque et ingentem cecidit
        Antiochum, Hannibalemque dirum;

Sed rusticorum mascula militum
Proles, Sabellis docta ligonibus
    Versare glebas, et severæ
        Matris ad arbitrium recisos

Portare fustes, sol ubi montium
Mutaret umbras et juga demeret
    Bobus fatigatis, amicum
        Tempus agens abeunte curru.

Damnosa quid non imminuit dies!
Ætas parentum, pejor avis, tulit
    Nos nequiores, mox daturos
        Progeniem vitiosiorem.

---

† "'Institor,' 'an agent, a trader in articles of dress or for the toilet.'"—YONGE. I have translated this "man-milliner," for there seems some kind of antithesis intended between the effeminate occupations of the "institor" and the rough manners of the shipmaster.

ODE VII.

TO ASTERIA.

This poem tells its own tale. It has that peculiar grace in which Horace is inimitable. Orelli says, "On account of its elegant pleasantry, and the mode in which the action is brought out into evidence— although the whole scene, and the three persons who play

Nay, Asteria, why weep'st thou for Gyges,
Whom, enriched with Bithynia's rich cargoes,
   The first sparkling zephyrs of spring
      Shall waft back to thee, constant as ever?

By the south wind on Oricus driven,
At the rise of the turbulent goat-star,
   Unsleeping, he weeps, through the night,
      The dull chill of his partnerless pillow.

But the agent of Chloë, his hostess,
Tells the youth that in her he has kindled
   A flame no less ardent than thine,
      In a thousand ways craftily tempting:

Warns him how the false consort of Prœtus
Duped her credulous lord, by feigned charges,
   Into plotting Bellerophon's death,
      For too chastely regarding his hostess.*

---

* Prœtus, believing the story of his wife Anteia, that Bellerophon had attempted to seduce her, but unwilling himself to slay

play their part in it, are pure poetic inventions—it may be classed among Horace's happiest poems." It is indeed a miniature lyrical comedy, and, slight though it be in substance, may be cited as an example of the skill with which Horace can give to a few stanzas the lively effect of a drama. The date is unknown, but is referred by some to A.U.C. 729.

CARM. VII.

Quid fles, Asterie, quem tibi candidi
Primo restituent vere Favonii
   Thyna merce beatum,
      Constantis juvenem fide,

Gygen? Ille Notis actus ad Oricum
Post insana Capræ sidera, frigidas
   Noctes non sine multis
      Insomnis lacrimis agit.

Atqui sollicitæ nuntius hospitæ,
Suspirare Chloën, et miseram tuis
   Dicens ignibus uri,
      Tentat mille vafer modis.

Ut Prœtum mulier perfida credulum
Falsis impulerit criminibus nimis
   Casto Bellerophonti
      Maturare necem, refert.*

his guest, sent him to his father-in-law Iobates, king in Lycia, with sealed letters, in which Iobates was requested to destroy the bearer.

Tells how Peleus, Hippolyte* slighted,
And was all but consigned to dark Hades;
   Then seeks to allure him by tales
      Teaching lessons for sinning in safety:

All in vain! To his words is thy true-love
Deaf as rocks to the breakers Icarian;
   But keep sharp look-out on thyself,
      Lest too charmed with thy neighbour Enipeus;

Though no rider so skilled and so noticed
Wheels a steed on the turf of the Campus; †
   No swimmer so lustily cleaves
      Rapid way down the stream of the Tuscan.

Make thy door fast at eve, never looking
Down the street if shrill fifes serenade thee;
   And be but more rigidly cold
      Whensoe'er he complains of thy coldness.

---

* This lady, otherwise called Astydamia, made the same charge against Peleus to her husband Acastor that Anteia did to Prœtus against Bellerophon, and for the same reason. Acastor, like Prœtus, having scruples of conscience which forbade him to slay his guest with his own hand, invited Peleus to hunt wild beasts in Mount Pelion; and when Peleus, overcome with fatigue,

Narrat pæne datum Pelea Tartaro,
Magnessam Hippolyten * dum fugit abstinens;
  Et peccare docentes
    Fallax historias movet:

Frustra: nam scopulis surdior Icari
Voces audit adhuc integer.   At tibi
  Ne vicinus Enipeus
    Plus justo placeat, cave;

Quamvis non alius flectere equum † sciens
Æque conspicitur gramine Martio,
  Nec quisquam citus æque
    Tusco denatat alveo.

Prima nocte domum claude; neque in vias
Sub cantu querulæ despice tibiæ:
  Et te sæpe vocanti
    Duram difficilis mane.

---

fell asleep on the mountain, Acastor concealed his sword, and left him alone and unarmed to be devoured by the beasts. Peleus on waking and searching for his sword was attacked by Centaurs, but saved by Chiron.

   † "Flectere equum." This was to wheel the horse round in a small circle.—MACLEANE.

ODE VIII.

TO MÆCENAS, ON THE ANNIVERSARY OF HORACE'S ESCAPE FROM THE FALLING TREE.

According to Franke, Horace's escape from the tree was in A.U.C. 728. Ritter places it in 724. This poem commemorates the anniversary of that accident.

Learned as thou art in lore of either language,*
Thou marvellest why these hymeneal Kalends
Of March† I keep—I, solitary Cælebs,
    Wherefore these flowerets?

This censer full of incense? this heaped fuel
On the live sod? Know that, escaped the death-blow
Of the dire tree, I a white goat to Bacchus
    Vowed, and feast-offerings.

The day, thus sacred, with the year returning,
Shall free from cork and all its pitch-sealed fastenings
That jar§ which first imbibed the smoke-reek under
    Tullus the Consul.

In honour of thy friend thus saved, Mæcenas,
Quaff brimming cups—a hundred be the number;
Let the gay lights watch with us for the morning,
    Noise and brawl banished.

---

* Viz., Greek and Latin, which, as the commentators observe, comprehended all the learning a Roman could well acquire.

Carm. VIII.

Martiis cælebs quid agam Kalendis,†
Quid velint flores et acerra thuris
Plena, miraris, positusque carbo in
    Cespite vivo,

Docte sermones utriusque linguæ? *
Voveram dulces epulas et album
Libero caprum, prope funeratus
    Arboris ictu.

Hic dies anno redeunte festus
Corticem adstrictum pice dimovebit
Amphoræ fumum § bibere institutæ
    Consule Tullo.

Sume, Mæcenas, cyathos amici
Sospitis centum, et vigiles lucernas
Perfer in lucem: procul omnis esto
    Clamor et ira.

---

† The Matronalia, in honour of Juno Lucina, were held in the March Kalends.

§ "Amphoræ fumum." The jar, or amphora, was kept in the apotheca, and ripened by the smoke from the bath below it. The pitch and cork which fastened in protected the wine itself from being smoked. The wine in the amphora now to be broached, dating back to Tullus the Consul, A.U.C. 683, would have been a year older than Horace himself.

Cast off the burden of a statesman's trouble,
Routed are Cotiso's fierce Dacian armies,
Mede wroth with Mede, upon fraternal slaughter,
    Wastes his wild fury.*

Subject to Rome, and curbed in tardy fetters,
The old Cantabrian foe on shores Hispanian;
Lo! the grim Scythians meditate retreating—
    Lax are their bow-strings.

As one who takes in private life his leisure,
A while forego the over-care for nations;
Leave things severe; life offers one glad moment—
    Seize it with gladness.

* The precise dates of these historical allusions are matters of controversy, and not possible to determine. By the Mede is meant the Parthian, distracted by the civil feuds between Phraates and Tiridates.

Mitte civiles super Urbe curas:
Occidit Daci Cotisonis agmen;
Medus infestus sibi luctuosis
    Dissidet armis:*

Servit Hispanæ vetus hostis oræ
Cantaber sera domitus catena:
Jam Scythæ laxo meditantur arcu
    Cedere campis.

Neglegens, ne qua populus laboret,
Parce privatus nimium cavere:
Dona præsentis cape lætus horæ, et
    Linque severa.

ODE IX.

THE RECONCILIATION.

"One of Buttmann's remarks with reference to this Ode is well worth quoting: 'The ancients had the skill to construct such poems so that each speech tells us by whom it is spoken; but we let the editors treat us all

HE.

"While I yet to thee was pleasing,
   While no dearer youth bestowed lavish arms round
         thy white neck,
Happy then, indeed, I flourished,
   Never Persian king* was blest with such riches as
         were mine."

SHE.

"While no other more inflamed thee,
   And below no Chloë's rank Lydia in thy heart was
         placed,
Glorious then did Lydia flourish,
   Roman Ilia's lofty name not so honoured as was
         mine."†

---

* "Persarum vigui rege beatior." The opposition between the lover's comparison in this stanza and the girl's in the next ("Romana vigui clarior Ilia") is this: The lover means that he was richer in her love than the wealthiest king; the girl that she

all our lives as schoolboys, and interline such dialogues after the fashion of our plays with the names. To their sedulity we are indebted for the alternation of the lyrical name Lydia with the name Horatius in this exquisite work of art; and yet even in an English poem we should be offended by seeing Collins at the side of Phyllis."—MACLEANE.

The poem itself is, perhaps, an imitation from the Greek. Macleane observes, "It is just such a subject as one might expect to find among the erotic poetry of the Greeks."

CARM. IX.

'Donec gratus eram tibi,
  Nec quisquam potior brachia candidæ
Cervici juvenis dabat,
  Persarum vigui rege beatior.'*

'Donec non alia magis
  Arsisti, neque erat Lydia post Chloën,
Multi Lydia nominis
  Romana vigui clarior Ilia.'†

(the humble freed-woman) was more honoured in his love than the most illustrious matron.

† Ilia, as the mother of Romulus, queen and priestess, stands here as the noblest type of Roman matrons, "Romanorum nobilissima."

He.

"O'er me now reigns Thracian Chloë,
   Skilled in notes of dulcet song and the science of
      the lute;
If my death her life could lengthen,
   So that Fate my darling spared, I without a fear
      could die."*

She.

"From a mutual torchlight kindled
   Is my flame for Calais, son of Thurian Ornytus,†
If my death his life could lengthen,
   So that Fate would spare the boy, I a double death
      would die!"

He.

"What if Venus fled—returning,
   Forced us two, dissevered now, back into her brazen
      yoke;
If I shook off auburn Chloë,
   And to Lydia, now shut out, opened once again
      the door?"

She.

"Than a star though he be fairer,
   Lighter thou than drifted cork—rougher thou than
      Hadrian wave,§
Yet how willingly I answer,
   'Tis with thee that I would live—gladly I with thee
      would die."

---

* "Si parcent animæ fata superstiti." "Animæ meæ" denotes a familiar expression of endearment, as in Cicero, ad. Fam. XIV. 14; and as the Italians still call their mistress, "Anima mia."

'Me nunc Thressa Chloë regit,
   Dulces docta modos, et citharæ sciens;
Pro qua non metuam mori,
   Si parcent animæ fata superstiti.'*

'Me torret face mutua
   Thurini Calaïs filius Ornyti;†
Pro quo bis patiar mori,
   Si parcent puero fata superstiti.'

'Quid, si prisca redit Venus
   Diductosque jugo cogit aëneo?
Si flava excutitur Chloë,
   Rejectæque patet janua Lydiæ?'

'Quamquam sidere pulchrior
   Ille est, tu levior cortice et improbo
Iracundior Hadria,§
   Tecum vivere amem, tecum obeam libens.'

† "Thurini Calaïs—Thressa Chloë." The alliteration between the names here selected seems studied. In making Chloe a Thracian and Calaïs the son of a Sybarite (Thurium, a town of Lucania, near the site of the ancient Sybaris), the poet perhaps insinuates that the lady who had replaced Lydia was somewhat too rude or masculine—the gentleman who had replaced the lover of the dialogue somewhat too soft and effeminate.

§ "Improbo — Hadria." Orelli interprets "improbo" by "*tobend*," "raging." The poets use the word "improbus" to imply anything in violent excess. Ritter, with perhaps over-subtlety, considers that the comparison to a cork refers, not to levity of temperament, but to the insignificant stature of the poet in contrast to the beauty of Calaïs.

ODE X.

TO LYCE.

This humorous ode belongs to a kind of serenade common enough with the Greeks, and is probably imitated

Didst thou drink the iced water of uttermost Don,
O Lyce! of some cruel savage the spouse,
Still, thy heart with compassion might think of me stretched
    Where the north winds are quartered outside of thy door.

Hark! the hinge of thy gate; hark! the plants in thy hall,[*]
With what dissonant howl they re-echo the blasts,
And, oh! how the chaste congelation of air
    Adds a yet purer coating of frost to the snow!

Lay the haughtiness hateful to Venus aside,
Lest the wheel should run back and the rope should be snapped,[†]
Thy good Tyrrhene father ne'er meant to beget
    A Penelope cruel to suitors in thee.

---

[*] "Nemus Inter pulchra satum tecta." Small trees were sometimes planted round the impluvium of a Roman house. This is the interpretation adopted by Orelli. Ritter contends that the line refers to one of the two sacred groves situated between the two heights of the Capitoline.

[†] "Ne currente retro funis eat rota." This line has been tortured to many interpretations. "Lest the wheel turn back and the

tated from a Greek original. There is no reason for supposing the Lyce whose cruelty is here complained of, to be identical with the Lyce who is lampooned in Book IV. Ode xiii.

CARM. X.

Extremum Tanain si biberes, Lyce,
Sævo nupta viro, me tamen asperas
Porrectum ante fores objicere incolis
    Plorares Aquilonibus.

Audis quo strepit janua, quo nemus
Inter pulchra satum tecta* remugiat
Ventis, et positas ut glaciet nives
    Puro numine Juppiter?

Ingratam Veneri pone superbiam,
Ne currente retro funis eat rota.†
Non te Penelopen difficilem procis
    Tyrrhenus genuit parens.

---

rope with it," is Orelli's, accepted by Macleane, who observes, the metaphor in that case is taken from a rope wound round a cylinder, which, being allowed to run back, the rope runs down, and the weight or thing attached goes with it. "The rope may break and the wheel run back," is the construction Macleane gives in his argument to the ode.

Ah! although thou art proof against presents and prayers,
And the pale-blue complexion of lovers disdained;
Nor ev'n bowed to revenge on the spouse led astray
    By a roving Pierian* less chaste than a Muse;

Yet, granting thy heart be not softer than oak,
Nor gentler than snakes—as a goddess, at least,
Spare the life of a suppliant! I am of flesh,
    And can bear not for ever this porch and that sleet.†

---

* "Pieria pellice," Macedonian lady of pleasure.—ORELLI, RITTER. There is some humour as well as wit in coupling "pellice" with an epithet so suggestive of an opposite idea.

† "Aquæ Cælestis patiens." The expression can scarcely apply to rain, since the night has been described as one of wind and frost:—

                  "Glaciet nives
           Puro numine Juppiter;"

"puro" being, as Macleane observes, "an epithet well suited to

BOOK III.—ODE X.

O quamvis neque te munera, nec preces,
Nec tinctus viola pallor amantium,
Nec vir Pieria pellice* saucius
    Curvat, supplicibus tuis

Parcas, nec rigida mollior æsculo
Nec Mauris animum mitior anguibus.
Non hoc semper erit liminis aut aquæ
    Cælestis patiens† latus.

---

a clear, frosty night." The wind would keep off the snow, but there might be gusty showers of sleety hail. Horace, however, no doubt, uses the expression in a general sense, such as the "floods of heaven," whether they be snow, rain, or sleet.

ODE XI.

TO THE LYRE.

"The common inscription, 'Ad Mercurium' (To Mercury), adopted by Bentley and others', is plainly wrong, and calculated to mislead. The inscription should

Mercury (for, tutored in thy lore, Amphion
Charmed into motion rocks by his sweet singing),
And thou, my lyre, with sevenfold chord resounding
    Measures not skill-less,

Albeit once, unmusical, unheeded,*
Now welcome both in banquet-halls and temples,
Teach me some strain resistlessly beguiling
    Lyde to listen.

Wild as the filly in its third year, frisking
Through the wide meadows, the least touch dismays
    her;
Never yet won, she views as saucy freedom
    Even the wooing.

But thou† hast power to lead away the tigers,
And in their train the forests; stay swift rivers;
Cerberus himself, dread jailer of dark thresholds,
    Soothed into meekness,

---

* "Nec loquax," *i.e.*, "canora,"—DILLENBURGER, ORELLI. Horace, though a born poet, if ever there was one—and telling us that even as an infant, when the doves covered him with bay and myrtle, he was marked out for the service of the Muses—does not

should be 'Ad testitudinem' (to the lyre or shell), if anything, for Mercury disappears after the first two verses. The miracles alluded to, except Amphion's, were those of Orpheus, and of the lyre in his hands, not Mercury's—which Orelli not perceiving, contradicts himself."—MACLEANE.

CARM. XI.

Mercuri, nam te docilis magistro
Movit Amphion lapides canendo,
Tuque, Testudo, resonare septem
    Callida nervis,

Nec loquax* olim neque grata, nunc et
Divitum mensis et amica templis;
Dic modos, Lyde quibus obstinatas
    Applicet aures:

Quæ, velut latis equa trima campis,
Ludit exsultim metuitque tangi,
Nuptiarum expers et adhuc protervo
    Cruda marito.

Tu† potes tigres comitesque silvas
Ducere, et rivos celeres morari;
Cessit immanis tibi blandienti
    Janitor aulæ,

disdain, here and elsewhere, to intimate that, if a born poet, he had taken very great pains to make himself a good one.

† "Thou" refers not to Mercury, but to the lyre—*i.e.*, symbolically to the power of song and music, as exercised by Orpheus.

Yielded to thy bland voice his hundred strongholds
Of fury-heads, each garrisoned with serpents,
And hushed the triple tongue in jaws whose breath-reek
    Tainted the hell-gloom;

The tortured lips of Tityos and Ixion
Reluctant smiled; awhile their urn stood thirsting
As paused the Danaids, to the charmer's music
    Dreamily listening.

Let Lyde hear the guilt of those stern virgins,
Hear, too, their well-known penance; doomed for ever
To toil at filling up a sieve-like vessel;
    Tell her how surely

Slow fates await such crimes,—though under Orcus;
Impious—for can impiety be greater?
Impious in giving to the sword their bridegrooms,
    Ruthlessly murdered.[*]

Amidst the many, One alone was worthy
The nuptial torch;—a maid, through all the ages,
By glorious falsehood to her perjured father,
    Nobly immortal.

---

[*] The old mythologists differ among themselves as to the fable of Danaus and the fate of his daughters. Horace here adopts the common story that Danaus, having reason to think that the fifty sons of his brother Ægyptus were plotting against him, fled with his fifty daughters from Libya (the domain assigned him by his father Belus, Ægyptus having Arabia), and ultimately became King of Argos. His nephews came to his new realm and demanded

Cerberus, quamvis furiale centum
Muniant angues caput ejus, atque
Spiritus teter saniesque manet
    Ore trilingui.

Quin et Ixion Tityosque voltu
Risit invito; stetit urna paullum
Sicca, dum grato Danai puellas
    Carmine mulces.

Audiat Lyde scelus atque notas
Virginum pœnas, et inane lymphæ
Dolium fundo pereuntis imo,
    Seraque fata,

Quæ manent culpas etiam sub Orco.
Impiæ, nam quid potuere majus?
Impiæ sponsos potuere duro
    Perdere ferro!*

Una de multis, face nuptiali
Digna, perjurum fuit in parentem
Splendide mendax, et in omne virgo
    Nobilis ævum,

his daughters in marriage. Danaus consented, but, in distrust or revenge, enjoined his daughters to murder their bridegrooms with the swords he gave them for that amiable purpose. One alone, Hypermnestra, spared her husband, Lynceus. According to the earlier writers, the Danaides were purified of their crime, and even married again. Later poets, deeming it perhaps more prudent to make a severe example of such dangerous bed-fellows, sent them to Orcus.

"Rise," to her youthful bridegroom, thus she whispered;
"Rise, lest there come, and whence thou dost suspect not,
Into thy lids the everlasting slumber!
 Baffle my father;

"Elude my blood-stained sisters—lionesses;
Each—woe is me!—her separate victim rending:
Of softer mould, I can nor strike nor pen thee
 Here, in these shambles!

"Let my sire load me with his barbarous fetters,
Wroth with the pitying love that spares a husband,
Or ship me outlawed to Numidian deserts!
 Be it so! Hasten!

"Go wheresoe'er fleet foot or sail can bear thee;
Blest be the auspice! Night and Venus favour!
Go, but remember me, and this sad story
 Carve on my tombstone!"*

---

* It is pleasant to think that the modern law of what is called "poetic justice," has a precedent in the final restoration of this young lady to the arms of the husband she had so mercifully spared. Probably she was the ugly one of the family, and less likely,

'Surge,' quæ dixit juveni marito,
'Surge, ne longus tibi somnus, unde
Non times, detur; socerum et scelestas
  Falle sorores;

Quæ velut nactæ vitulos leænæ
Singulos eheu lacerant: ego illis
Mollior nec te feriam neque intra
  Claustra tenebo.

Me pater sævis oneret catenis,
Quod viro clemens misero peperci;
Me vel extremos Numidarum in agros
  Classe releget.

I, pedes quo te rapiunt et auræ,
Dum favet nox et Venus: I secundo
Omine, et nostri memorem sepulcro
  Scalpe querelam.'*

if she killed one husband, to find another. Ovid's Epistle of Hypermnestra to Lynceus, supposed to be written while imprisoned by her father, is much indebted to Horace's lines. But perhaps both poets borrowed from a common source which is lost to modern discoverers.

ODE XII.

NEOBULE'S SOLILOQUY.

Most of the earlier commentators took it for granted that the poet is here addressing Neobule. Dillenburger, Orelli, and Macleane prefer to consider that Neobule is throughout the ode addressing herself. The poem is,

How unhappy the lot of poor girls; neither play to
    their fancies in love,
Neither balm for their sorrows in wine! frightened out
    of their souls by the lash
    In the tongue of some testy relation. *

Neobule, winged Love has flown off with thy spindles
    and basket of wools!
And thy studious delight in the toils of Minerva is
    chased from thy heart
    By young Hebrus, the bright Liparæan.

Hardy swimmer in Tiber to plunge gleaming shoulders
    anointed with oil!
Sure, Bellerophon rode not so well; as a boxer no arm
    is so strong;
    And no foot is so fleet as a runner.

Skiful marksman, when over the champaign the hounds
    drive and scatter the deer,
To select the right stag for his dart; and as nimble to
    start the wild boar,
    Lurking grim in the dense forest-thicket.

is, perhaps, more or less imitated from one by Alcæus, of which only a single verse is preserved. The metre of the ode has given much trouble to commentators, especially to those who insist upon the theory that all Horace's odes are reducible to quatrain stanzas, while this ode is in a stanza of three lines, according to the authority of MSS. (with the exception of the Turinese one). An attempt to remodel it into quatrain will be found in Orelli's excursus to the ode, and is adopted by Yonge in his edition.

CARM. XII.

Miserarum est neque amori dare ludum, neque dulci
Mala vino lavere, aut exanimari metuentes
    Patruæ verbera linguæ.*

Tibi qualum Cythereæ puer ales, tibi telas
Operosæque Minervæ studium aufert, Neobule,
    Liparæi nitor Hebri,

Simul unctos Tiberinis humeros lavit in undis,
Eques ipso melior Bellerophonte, neque pugno
    Neque segni pede victus;

Catus idem per apertum fugientes agitato
Grege cervos jaculari, et celer alto latitantem
    Fruticeto excipere aprum.

---

* Literally "uncle." "Uncles," Torrentius observes, "had considerable power over their nephews and nieces by the Roman law, and, being less indulgent than fathers, their severity passed into a proverb."

ODE XIII.

TO THE BANDUSIAN FOUNTAIN.

The site of this fountain has been a matter of controversy, interesting to those who seek to ascertain the localities of places endeared to them by the poets. Acron and others assumed it to be in the neighbourhood of Horace's Sabine home, and identify it with the rivulet of Digentia (Licenza). It is, however, generally now agreed, upon what appears sufficiently competent authority, that Bandusia was in Horace's native soil, about six miles from the site of Venusia (Dillenburger,

Fount of Bandusia, more lucid than crystal,
Worthy of honeyed wine, not without flowers,
   I will give thee to-morrow a kid,
      Whose front, with the budded horn swelling,

Predicts to his future life Venus and battles;
Vainly! The lymph of thy cold running waters
   He shall tinge with the red of his blood,
      Fated child of the frolicsome people!

The scorch of the dog-star's fell season forbears thee;
Ever friendly to grant the sweet boon of thy coolness
   To the wild flocks that wander around,
      And the oxen that reek from the harrow.

(Dillenburger, Orelli, Macleane). If so, it is conjectured that the poem would have been written in earlier life, when Horace revisited his native spot—perhaps A.U.C. 717—since it is held scarcely probable that he would have thought of consecrating the fountain in Venusia, when he was settled in the remote district of his Sabine farm. It may, however, be likely enough, as Tate contends (Horat. Restit. p. 88), that Horace transferred the name, endeared to him by early association, to the spring near his later home. Yonge suggests the query, "Was Bandusia the name of the place, or of the presiding nymph of the fountain?"— See Orelli's full and very elegant note on this subject.

CARM. XIII.

O fons Bandusiæ, splendidior vitro,
Dulci digne mero non sine floribus,
   Cras donaberis hædo,
      Cui frons turgida cornibus

Primis et venerem et prœlia destinat;
Frustra: nam gelidos inficiet tibi
   Rubro sanguine rivos
      Lascivi suboles gregis.

Te flagrantis atrox hora Caniculæ
Nescit tangere; tu frigus amabile
   Fessis vomere tauris
      Præbes, et pecori vago.

I will give thee high rank and renown among fountains,
When I sing of the ilex o'erspreading the hollows
  Of rocks, whence, in musical fall,*
    Leap thy garrulous silvery waters.

* "Me dicente cavis impositam ilicem Saxis"—the cavern overshadowed with the ilex from which the fountain gushes.—ORELLI.

Fies nobilium tu quoque fontium,
Me dicente cavis impositam ilicem
　Saxis,* unde loquaces
　　Lymphæ desiliunt tuæ.

ODE XIV.

"Composed at the close of the Cantabrian war, A. U. C. 729, when Augustus's return was expected, or on his return the following year."—MACLEANE.

In
Joy, O ye people! it was said that Cæsar
Went forth like Hercules, in quest of laurels
Bought but by death; now home from shores Hispanian
    Comes he back victor.

Let her whose joy in her sole lord is centred*
Join, in thanksgivings due, the glad procession—
Join with the sister of our glorious chieftain—
    Join with the mothers,

Chastely adorned by sacrificial fillets †—
Mothers of children now no more imperilled;
Youths and young brides hush, at such time ill-omened,
    Each lighter whisper.

Truly to me this holiday is sacred,
And its bright sunshine chases cloudy troubles.
I fear nor open brawl nor stealthy murder, §
    Cæsar yet living!

---

* "Unico gaudens mulier marito." See Orelli's note on "unico," which some have interpreted in the sense of "unique" or "peerless;" Dillenburger, as "dear" or "beloved."

† Worn by the Roman matrons to distinguish them from freed women.

In noticing the critical animadversions on this ode "as unequal to the occasion," Macleane observes justly that "it was evidently only a private affair." The familiar lightness of the concluding stanzas would indicate a merry-making kept with a few personal friends.

CARM. XIV.

Herculis ritu modo dictus, O Plebs,
Morte venalem petiisse laurum,
Caesar Hispana repetit Penates
    Victor ab ora.

Unico gaudens mulier marito *
Prodeat, justis operata sacris;
Et soror clari ducis, et decorae
    Supplice vitta

Virginum matres, juvenumque nuper †
Sospitum. Vos, O pueri et puellae
Jam virum expertae, male ominatis
    Parcite verbis.

Hic dies vere mihi festus atras
Eximet curas; ego nec tumultum,
Nec mori per vim metuam, § tenente
    Caesare terras.

§ "Nec tumultum,
Nec mori per vim metuam."

"Tumultum" here evidently means "intestine feud" or "popular outbreak;" "vim," "assassination" or "personal violence." With Caesar is identified the prevailing security of law.

Up, boy, and bring the perfume and the garlands,
And wine that to the Marsian war bears witness,
If one jar, baffling Spartacus the Rover,
    Somewhere lurks hidden.*

Go, and bid silver-tongued Neæra hasten,
Binding in Spartan knot her locks myrrh-scented; †
But, if obstructed by that brute her porter,
    Quietly come back.

Nothing cools fiery spirits like a grey hair;
In every quarrel 'tis your sure peacemaker;
In my hot youth, when Plancus was the consul,
    I was less patient. §

---

* "The Marsic or Social war was continued from A. U. C. 663 to 665; and the Servile war, headed by Spartacus, lasted from A. U. C. 681 to 683; therefore the wine Horace wanted would have been sixty-five years old at least. There seems to have been something remarkable in the vintage of that period, so as to make it proverbial; for Juvenal, one hundred years afterwards, speaking of the selfish gentleman who keeps his best wine for his own drinking, says:—

'Ipse capillato diffusum consule potat,
Calcatamque tenet bellis socialibus uvam.'"
—S. V. 30, 89.—MACLEANE.

BOOK III.—ODE XIV.

I, pete unguentum, puer, et coronas,
Et cadum Marsi memorem duelli,
Spartacum* si qua potuit vagantem
    Fallere testa.

Dic et argutæ properet Neæræ
Myrrheum nodo cohibere crinem; †
Si per invisum mora janitorem
    Fiet, abito.

Lenit albescens animos capillus
Litium et rixæ cupidos protervæ;
Non ego hoc ferrem calidus juventa, §
    Consule Planco.

---

† "Myrrheum crinem." The scholiasts interpreted this expression "myrrh-coloured." Orelli and other recent commentators support the interpretation "myrrh-scented."

§ *I.e.*, when Horace was in his twenty-third year.

ODE XV.

ON AN OLD WOMAN AFFECTING YOUTH.

The names in this poem are, of course, fictitious, and the satire itself is of very general application even in the present day. Its date is undiscoverable.

Mend thy life—it is time; cease such pains to be vile,
    Flaunting wife of the indigent Ibycus;
Fitter far for the grave, do not gambol with girls,
    Interspersing a cloud 'mid the galaxy.

That which Pholoë thy daughter may suit well enough,
    In thee, hoary Chloris, is horrible:*
'Tis permitted to her to besiege the young rakes
    In their homes, with much greater propriety:

No Bacchante the timbrel excites with its clash,
    Than that daughter of thine can be livelier;
And now that with Nothus she's fallen in love,
    Not a roe on the hills is more frolicsome.

What becomes thee the best is a warm woollen dress;
    Get thee fleeces from famous Luceria;†
What become thee the least are the lute and the rose,
    And the cask tippled dry with young rioters.

---

* "Anus cum ludit, Morti delicias facit."—P. SYRUS.

† A town in Apulia now called Lucera. In its neighbourhood was one of the largest tracts of public pasture-land. The wools of Luceria were celebrated.

Carm. XV.

Uxor pauperis Ibyci,
   Tandem nequitiæ fige modum tuæ,
Famosisque laboribus:
   Maturo propior desine funeri

Inter ludere virgines,
   Et stellis nebulam spargere candidis.
Non, si quid Pholoën satis,
   Et te, Chlori, decet:* filia rectius

Expugnat juvenum domos,
   Pulso Thyias uti concita tympano.
Illam cogit amor Nothi
   Lascivæ similem ludere capreæ:

Te lanæ prope nobilem
   Tonsæ Luceriam,† non citharæ, decent
Nec flos purpureus rosæ,
   Nec poti, vetulam, fæce tenus cadi.

ODE XVI.

GOLD THE CORRUPTOR.

This ode is among Horace's most striking variations of the moral he so frequently preaches—content *versus* gold. But here he does full justice to the power of gold

The brazen tower, the solid doors,* the vigil
Of dismal watch-dogs sentried night and day,
   Might have sufficed to guard
     From midnight loves imprisoned Danaë;

But Jove and Venus laughed to scorn Acrisius,
The timorous jailer of the hidden maid, †
   Opening at once sure way,
     The god transformed himself into—a Bribe.

More subtle than the flash of the forked lightning,
Gold glides amidst the armèd satellites;
   More potent than Jove's bolt,
     Gold through the walls of granite bursts its way:

So fell the Argive Augur with his kindred, §
Gain, tempting one, whelmed in destruction all;

---

* "Robustæque fores." Orelli suggests "firmissimæ," and objects, not without fine critical taste, to the interpretation of Forcellini and others—viz., "*oaken* doors," as a descent in poetic expression, just after insisting on "brazen tower." Certainly, in line 9, Ode III., "Illi robur et æs triplex," "robur" comes first.

† Acrisius shut up his daughter in a brazen tower from fear of the oracle, who had predicted that she should bear him a son who

gold as the corruptor. I have not adopted for this ode the forms of metre I have elsewhere employed for rendering odes in the same measure (Asclepiadean, with a Glyconean in the 4th line), but one by which I have not unfrequently rendered the Alcaic stanza, with the slight variation of a monosyllabic termination in the second verse, while the termination of the first verse is dissyllabic.

Carm. XVI.

Inclusam Danaën turris aënea
Robustæque fores,* et vigilum canum
Tristes excubiæ munierant satis
    Nocturnis ab adulteris,

Si non Acrisium virginis abditæ †
Custodem pavidum, Juppiter et Venus
Risissent: fore enim tutum iter et patens
    Converso in pretium deo.

Aurum per medios ire satellites,
Et perrumpere amat saxa potentius
Ictu fulmineo: concidit auguris
    Argivi § domus ob lucrum

---

would cause his death. He is therefore timorous or panic-stricken (pavidus) because of the oracle.

§ Amphiaraus; his wife Eriphyle, bribed by her brother Polynices, persuaded him to join in the siege of Thebes. There he fell, ordering his sons to put their mother to death. Alcmæon obeyed, and finally perished himself in attempting to get the gold necklace with which Eriphyle had been bribed.

>The man of Macedon *
>>By gifts cleft gates, by gifts sapped rival thrones—

Gifts baited for fierce admirals, net whole navies; †
Care grows with wealth, with wealth the greed for more.
>O my Mæcenas! gem
>>Of Roman knighthood, § ever have I feared

To lift a crest above the crowd conspicuous—
Rightly; the more man shall deny himself,
>The more shall gods bestow.
>>I do not side with wealth, but, lightly armed,

Bound o'er the lines, deserting to Contentment;
Owner more grand in means the rich despise,
>Than were I said to hide,
>>In mine own granaries, all Apulia yields

Her toiling sons, want-pinched amidst heaped plenty:—
A brooklet pure, some roods of woodland cool,
>Faith in crops, sure if small—
>>Are a lot happier, though he knows it not,

Than his who glitters in the spoils of Afric.
Though not for me toil the Calabrian bees,
>Nor wines in Formian jars
>>Languish their fire in length of years away,

---

* Philip of Macedon.

† This is held to refer to Menas, *alias* Menodorus, commander of Sextus Pompeius's fleet. He deserted from Pompeius to Augustus, then again to Pompeius, and again to Augustus. He had been freed-man to C. M. Pompeius.

§ "Mæcenas, equitum decus." By this significant reference to

BOOK III.—ODE XVI.

Demersa exitio; diffidit urbium
Portas vir Macedo,* et subruit æmulos
Reges muneribus; munera navium
    Sævos illaqueant duces.†

Crescentem sequitur cura pecuniam
Majorumque fames. Jure perhorrui
Late conspicuum tollere verticem,
    Mæcenas, equitum decus. §

Quanto quisque sibi plura negaverit,
Ab dis plura feret. Nil cupientium
Nudus castra peto, et transfuga divitum
    Partes linquere gestio,

Contemptæ dominus splendidior rei,
Quam si, quidquid arat impiger Apulus,
Occultare meis dicerer horreis,
    Magnas inter opes inops.

Puræ rivus aquæ, silvaque jugerum
Paucorum, et segetis certa fides meæ,
Fulgentem imperio fertilis Africæ
    Fallit sorte beatior.

Quamquam nec Calabræ mella ferunt apes,
Nec Læstrygonia Bacchus in amphora
Languescit mihi, nec pinguia Gallicis
    Crescunt vellera pascuis,

Mæcenas as the ornament of knighthood, Horace associates Mæcenas with himself in the philosophy of contentment—Mæcenas, having always remained in the equestrian order, to which he was born, declining promotion to the senatorial.

Nor fleecy wools gain weight in Gallic pastures,
Yet Penury keeps aloof; nor, lacked I more,
   More wouldst thou me deny:
      Widening my means by narrowing my desires,

I shall have ampler margin for true riches
Than if to Lydia adding Phrygian realms.
   Who covets much, much wants;
      God gives most kindly giving just enough.

Importuna tamen Pauperies abest;
Nec, si plura velim, tu dare deneges.
Contracto melius parva cupidine
　　Vectigalia porrigam,

Quam si Mygdoniis regnum Alyattei
Campis continuem.　Multa petentibus
Desunt multa: bene est, cui Deus obtulit
　　Parca, quod satis est, manu.

ODE XVII.

TO L. ÆLIUS LAMIA.

This personage was the son of the L. Æ. Lamia who supported Cicero in the suppression of the Catiline conspiracy, and appears during the civil wars to have espoused the party of Cæsar. Horace's friend was consul A. D. 3; afterwards appointed by Tiberius governor of Syria, but not allowed to enter on the administration of the province. He became, A. D. 32, "Prætectus Urbi," and died the following year. Mitscherlich says: "His own good sense will easily show any well-bred

Noble Ælius, whose house hath its rise in that Lamus
From whom both the first and the later descendants
   (As attesting memorials* record)
     The great name of Lamia inherit,

Thou canst trace back, indeed, to an absolute monarch,
Holding sway, it is said, over Formia's walled ramparts,
   And the waters of Liris, that flow
     Into grassy domains of Marica.

To-morrow the east wind shall send us a tempest,
Which—if true be the crow, that old seer of foul weather—
   Shall strew in the grove many leaves;
     On the shore,† many profitless sea-weeds.

---

* "Per memores—fastos." "Family records," not the "fasti consulares."—MACLEANE.

well-bred gentleman (urbanum) that Horace here, in a well-bred, gentlemanlike way, offers himself as a guest; in plain words, hints that Lamia should ask him to dine." On which the commentator in Orelli observes, with much feeling asperity: "In the whole poem there is not a vestige of this sort of gentlemanlike good-breeding, if gentlemanlike good-breeding it be, which it is permitted vehemently to doubt." Evidently the commentator is an Italian. A gentleman of that country would certainly dispute the good-breeding of any friend offering to drop in at dinner.

Carm. XVII.

Æli, vetusto nobilis ab Lamo,
Quando et priores hinc Lamias ferunt
  Denominatos, et nepotum
    Per memores genus omne fastos; *

Auctore ab illo ducis originem,
Qui Formiarum mœnia dicitur
  Princeps et innantem Maricæ
    Litoribus tenuisse Lirim, †

Late tyrannus: cras foliis nemus
Multis et alga litus inutili
  Demissa tempestas ab Euro
    Sternet, aquæ nisi fallit augur

---

† The shore of Minturna, on the borders of Latium and Campania, where the nymph Marica was worshipped.

While thou canst, then, protect from the rains the dry
    faggots;
Spend to-morrow in resting thyself and thy household;
  Feast thy genius with wine—but not mixed;
    And do not forget a young porker.

Annosa cornix. Dum potis, aridum
Compone lignum: cras Genium mero
  Curabis et porco bimestri,
    Cum famulis operum solutis.

ODE XVIII.

TO FAUNUS.

Faunus was not a stationary divinity. He was supposed to come in the spring, and depart after the celebration of his festival in December. From "parvis alumnis" (translated "young weanlings"), we may suppose this ode was written in spring.—MACLEANE.
Ritter

Faunus, thou lover of coy nymphs who fly thee,
Enter my bounds, and fields that slope to sunlight;
Enter them gently; and depart, propitious
    To my young weanlings,

If tender kid, when the year rounds, be offered;
If to the bowl, Venus's boon companion,
Fail not libation due!*—With ample incense
    Steams thine old altar,

Loose strays the herd on grassy meads disporting,
What time December's Nones bring back thy feast-day;
Blithe, o'er the fields, streams forth the idling hamlet,
    Freed—with its oxen.

---

* "Si tener pleno cadit hædus anno,
  Larga nec desunt Veneris sodali
  Vina crateræ. Vetus ara multo
    Fumat odore," &c.

As I have here adopted a novelty in the punctuation, suggested by Macleane, it is well to subjoin his reasons for the innovation. "I have not followed the usual punctuation, which makes 'fumat' depend upon 'si,' with a comma at 'crateræ,' and a period at

Ritter denies that by "parvis alumnis" young animals are meant; and contends that the words refer to young plants, transferred from the nursery to fields or orchards. Ritter also dissents from the general interpretation, which I have followed, that "Veneris sodali" is to be coupled with "craterae." According to him, the companion of Venus is Faunus, the lover of the Nymphs, and not the wine-bowl.

Carm. XVIII.

Faune, Nympharum fugientum amator,
Per meos fines et aprica rura
Lenis incedas abeasque parvis
    Æquus alumnis;

Si tener pleno cadit hædus anno,
Larga nec desunt Veneris sodali
Vina craterae. Vetus ara multo
    Fumat odore,*

Ludit herboso pecus omne campo,
Cum tibi Nonae redeunt Decembres;
Festus in pratis vacat otioso
    Cum bove pagus;

---

* 'odore.' Horace claims the protection of Faunus for his lambs in the spring on the ground of his due observance of the rights of December, which he then goes on to describe. 'Pleno anno' means at the end of the year when the Faunalia took place." Therefore the division in the poem at which, after the invitation to Faunus in the spring, Horace passes on to describe the festival in the winter, is more intelligible, and far less abrupt, by commencing it with the sacrifice on the altar.

Fearless the lambs behold the wolf prowl near them;
The woodland strews its leaves before thy footstep;
And on his hard task-mistress Earth, exulting,
   Thrice stamps the delver!*

    * "Gaudet invisam pepulisse fossor
        Ter pede terram."

"'Fossor' is put generally, I imagine, for a labouring husbandman, who may be supposed to have no love for the earth that he digs for another."—MACLEANE. This triple stamp is a dancing measure, which is likened to the anapæst, where two feet are short and one long. Macleane quotes Sir John Davies's poem (Orchestra) in explanation of this measure—

    "And still their feet an anapæst do sound," &c.

But it is perhaps best understood by any one who happens to have

Inter audaces lupus errat agnos;
Spargit agrestes tibi silva frondes;
Gaudet invisam pepulisse fossor
　　Ter pede terram.*

learned, in the old-fashioned hornpipe, that step familiarly called "toe, heel, and cloe,"—touching the ground lightly with the toe, next with the heel, and then bringing down the whole sole of the foot with a stamp. I have seen that step, or something very like it, performed in a village dance in the south of Italy.

ODE XIX.

TO TELEPHUS.—IN HONOUR OF MURENA'S INSTALLATION IN THE COLLEGE OF AUGURS.

A. Terentius Varro Murena, adopted by A. Terentius Varro, whose name he took, according to custom, subdued the Salassi, an Alpine tribe, and divided their territory among Prætorian soldiers, who founded the town of Augusta, now Aosta. He was named Consul Suffectus

You tell us how long after Inachus flourished
King Codrus, who feared not to die for his country;
   What noble descendants from Æacus sprung,
      What battles were fought under Ilion the sacred;

But you say not a word upon things more important—
What price one must pay for a cask of old Chian?
   Baths,* rooms—where and whose? What the moment to thaw
      These frost-bitten limbs in the sunshine of supper?

Ho, boy, there, a cup!† Brim it full for the New Moon!
Ho, boy, there, a cup! Brim it full for the Midnight!

---

* "Quis aquam temperet ignibus." Orelli considers this refers to the water to be warmed for the baths; Ritter, to the water to be warmed for admixture with wine. I have adopted the former interpretation, though I think it doubtful.

BOOK III.—ODE XIX.

Suffectus for B.C. 23. In B.C. 22 he was involved in the conspiracy of Fannius Cæpio against the life of Augustus, and, though his guilt seems doubtful, executed. This is the same person whom Horace addresses under the name Licinius, Book II. Ode x., "Rectius vives Licini," &c. The metre in the original is the second Asclepiadean; but I have found it easier to preserve fidelity to the sense and spirit of the poem by employing one of the varieties of rhythm which I have appropriated to the Alcaic.

CARM. XIX.

Quantum distet ab Inacho
   Codrus, pro patria non timidus mori,
Narras, et genus Æaci,
   Et pugnata sacro bella sub Ilio:

Quo Chium pretio cadum
   Mercemur, quis aquam temperet ignibus,*
Quo præbente domum et quota
   Pelignis caream frigoribus, taces.

†Da Lunæ propere novæ,
   Da Noctis mediæ, da, puer, auguris

---

† "Here, in a kind of phantasy, the poet transports himself with Telephus into the midst of the entertainment."—ORELLI.

Ho, boy, there, a cup! Brim it full—to the health
Of him we would honour!—Murena the Augur.

Proportioned the bowls are to three or nine measures,
As each man likes best;* the true poet will ever
    Suit his to the odd-numbered Muses, and quaff
        Thrice three in the rapture the Nine give to
            brimmers.

But the Grace, with her twin naked sisters, shuns quarrel,
And to more than three measures refuses her sanction.
    Ho! ho! what a joy to go mad for a time!
        Why on earth stops the breath of that fife Berecyn-
            thian?

And why is that harp so unsocially silent,
And the lively Pandean pipe idly suspended?
    Quick, roses—and more! Let it rain with the rose!
        There is nothing I hate like the hand of a niggard.

Let the noise of our mirth split the ears of old Lycus.
He is envious—our riot shall gorge him with envy.
    The ears of our neighbour, his wife, let it reach.
        No wife could suit less the grey hairs of old Lycus.†

---

* "Tribus aut novem
Miscentur cyathis pocula commodis."

"The 'cyathus' was a ladle with which the drink was passed from the mixing-bowl to the drinking-cup. The ladle was of certain capacity, and twelve 'cyathi' went to the Sextarius. Horace says, in effect, 'Let the wine be mixed in the proportion of three cyathi of wine to nine of water, or of nine of wine to three of water.' . .

Murenæ: tribus aut novem
  Miscentur cyathis pocula commodis. *

Qui Musas amat impares,
  Ternos ter cyathos attonitus petet
Vates; tres prohibet supra
  Rixarum metuens tangere Gratia,

Nudis juncta sororibus.
  Insanire juvat: cur Berecyntiæ
Cessant flamina tibiæ?
  Cur pendet tacita fistula cum lyra?

Parcentes ego dexteras
  Odi: sparge rosas; audiat invidus
Dementem strepitum Lycus
  Et vicina seni non habilis Lyco.†

'Commodis,' 'fit and proper,'—'cyathi,' that is, 'bumpers.'"—MACLEANE. The above seems the best and most intelligible interpretation of a passage in which, if conjectures were cyathi, the commentators would have greatly exceeded the number allowed to the nine Muses.

† The graduated process of a drinking-bout is most naturally simulated in these verses. First stage, the amiable expansion of heart in the friendly toast—the toleration of differing tastes;—each man may drink as much as he likes. Secondly, the consciousness of getting drunk, and thinking it a fine thing;—joy to go mad. Thirdly, the craving for noise;—let the band strike up. Fourthly, a desire for something cool;—roses in ancient Rome—soda-water in modern England. Fifthly, the combative stage;—aggressive insult to poor old Lycus. Sixthly, the maudlin stage, soft and tender;—complimentary to Telephus, and confidingly pathetic as to his own less fortunate love-affairs.

Thee, O Telephus, radiant with locks of thick cluster,
Thee, with face like the star of the eve at its clearest,
    Budded Rhode is courting; I too am on fire,
        But me Glycera keeps in the flames burning slowly.*

* Commentators have endeavoured to create a puzzle even here, where the meaning appears very obvious. Rhode runs after you (petit), who are so handsome—Glycera does not run after me, but

Spissa te nitidum coma,
   Puro te similem, Telephe, Vespero,
Tempestiva petit Rhode:
   Me lentus Glycerae torret amor meae.*

keeps me languishing; the sense is consistent with the tone, half envious, half sarcastic, with which the poet always speaks of Telephus, the typical beauty-man and lady-killer.

ODE XX.—OMITTED.

ODE XXI.

TO MY CASK.

This poem appears composed in honour of some occasion in which Horace entertained the famous L. Valerius Messala Corvinus. No man in that great age was more remarkable for the variety of his accomplishments than this Corvinus. Sprung from one of the greatest consular families, he espoused the senatorian party in the civil wars, and attached himself especially to

Coeval with me, born when Manlius was consul,
Whatsoe'er the effects of thy life, while in action—
   Spleen or mirth, angry brawl or wild love,
     Or, O gentle cask,* ready slumber—

Under what head soe'er there be entered account of †
The grapes thou hast kept since in Massicus gathered,
   Thou art worth being roused on a day
     Of good fortune; descend§ for Corvinus

---

* "Pia testa." The exact meaning of "pia" here has given rise to much critical disputation. Macleane says he knows no better translation than Francis's "gentle cask," for the meaning is to be derived from its connection with "facilem somnum." Yonge adopts the same interpretation, "gentle, kindly,"—observing "it would be 'impia' if producing 'querelas, rixas,'" &c. I have translated "testa" cask, as a word familiar to the English reader, but it here properly means the amphora, a vessel into which the wine was, as we should say, bottled.

to Cassius. He held the third place in the command of the Republican army, and at Philippi turned Augustus's flank, stormed his camp, and nearly took him prisoner. Subsequently he made terms with Antony, whom he left for Augustus, after Antony's league with Cleopatra—and at Actium commanded the centre of the fleet with great distinction. Besides his eminence as a commander and a statesman, he was conspicuous as an orator, a wit, a historian, and a grammarian. He also wrote poetry.—See Smith's Dictionary for fuller details of his life, art. "Messala."

CARM. XXI.

O nata mecum consule Manlio,
Seu tu querelas, sive geris jocos
   Seu rixam et insanos amores,
     Seu facilem, pia testa,* somnum,

Quocunque lectum nomine† Massicum
Servas, moveri digna bono die,
   Descende,§ Corvino jubente
     Promere languidiora vina.

† "Quocunque nomine," "on whatever account." On the technical meaning of "nomen," signifying "an entry in an account," see Mr Long's note on Cicero in Verr. II, 1, 38. "'Lectum,' which Forcellini interprets 'selected,' rather applies to the gathering of the grape from which the wine was made. Massic wine was from Mons Massicus in Campania."—MACLEANE.

§ "Descend"—*i.e.*, descend from the place where it was kept (apotheca), in the upper part of the house.

Asking wines by age mellowed! He will not neglect
    thee,
All imbued though he be with Socratical maxims.
  Father Cato, full often, 'tis said,
    Warmed his virtue with wine undiluted.*

Thou givest a soft-pricking spur to the sluggish,
Makest gentle the harsh, and confiding the cautious.
  Chasing care from the brows of the wise,
    Thou unlockest their hearts to Lyæus.†

Hope and nerve thou restorest to minds worn and
    harassed,
Add'st the horn that exalts to the front of the beggar;
  Fresh from thee he could face down a king,
    Fresh from thee, brave the charge of an army.

Thee, shall Liber and Venus, if Venus come merry,
And the Graces, reluctant their bond to dissever,
  And the living lights gaily prolong,
    Till the stars fly from Phœbus returning.

---

  * Undiluted—"mero."
  † "Retegis Lyæo." "The dative case, 'to' Lyæus, appears here to be employed rather than the ablative."—ORELLI.

Non ille, quamquam Socraticis madet
Sermonibus, te negleget horridus:
   Narratur et prisci Catonis
     Sæpe mero* caluisse virtus.

Tu lene tormentum ingenio admoves
Plerumque duro; tu sapientium
   Curas et arcanum jocoso
     Consilium retegis Lyæo; †

Tu spem reducis mentibus anxiis,
Viresque et addis cornua pauperi,
   Post te neque iratos trementi
     Regum apices, neque militum arma.

Te Liber et, si læta aderit, Venus,
Segnesque nodum solvere Gratiæ,
   Vivæque producent lucernæ,
     Dum rediens fugat astra Phœbus.

ODE XXII.

VOTIVE INSCRIPTION TO DIANA.

Nothing more need be said of this ode than that it is one of the votive inscriptions common among the ancients, and that a pine-tree would be very fittingly dedicated to Diana. The attempts made to extract a story

Guardian of mountain-peaks, and forests—Virgin,
Goddess triformed—who, thrice invoked, benignly
Dost hear young mothers in their hour of travail,
    And from death save them;

Thine be this pine which overhangs my villa,
To which each closing year shall be devoted
A youthful boar, of sidelong thrusts indulging
    Vain meditations.

story out of the occasion and the offering are preposterous. That which is chiefly noticeable in this and other poems by Horace, more or less similar, is the rare and admirable merit of terseness. The poet has sufficient reliance on himself to be sure that, however briefly and simply he expresses himself on a subject to which brevity and simplicity belong, his unmistakable mark will appear on the work.

CARM. XXII.

Montium custos nemorumque, Virgo,
Quæ laborantes utero puellas
Ter vocata audis, adimisque leto,
    Diva triformis:

Imminens villæ tua pinus esto,
Quam per exactos ego lætus annos
Verris obliquum meditantis ictum
    Sanguine donem.

ODE XXIII.

TO PHIDYLE.

Jani and other commentators have supposed the Phidyle here addressed to be Horace's country house-keeper,

If with each new-born moon thou lift to Heaven thy
    suppliant hands,
If with some grains of frankincense, fresh corn, and
    flesh of swine,
  My rustic Phidyle, thy rites
    Appease thy simple Lares,

Thy fruitful vines shall neither feel the south wind's
    poisoned breath,*
Nor mildew blight to sterile dearth thy harvests in the
    ear,
  Nor appled autumn's sicklied airs
    Infect thy tender weanlings.

Let victims whose devoted blood shall tinge the Pontiff's
    axe
Pasture on snow-clad Algidus, mid oak and ilex groves,
  Or, fattening fast on Alban meads,
    Grow ripe for pompous slaughter:†

---

* "Pestilentem Africum," the sirocco.—ORELLI.

† The flocks and herds that belonged to the College of Pontiffs were fed on Algidus and the meadows of Alba Longa.

keeper, and that Horace in this ode answers some complaint of hers that her master did not permit her to sacrifice in a manner sufficiently handsome. Orelli observes that Phidyle could not be Horace's servant, for she is represented as sacrificing according to her own choice and will. But this no servant could do: the act of sacrifice for the whole family belonged exclusively to the head of the establishment. The ode, if addressed to any individual at all—which it probably was not—would have been addressed, therefore, to some mistress of a plain country household.

Carm. XXIII.

Cælo supinas si tuleris manus
Nascente Luna, rustica Phidyle,
  Si thure placaris et horna
    Fruge Lares, avidaque porca,

Nec pestilentem sentiet Africum*
Fecunda vitis, nec sterilem seges
  Robiginem, aut dulces alumni
    Pomifero grave tempus anno.

Nam, quæ nivali pascitur Algido
Devota quercus inter et ilices,
  Aut crescit Albanis in herbis,†
    Victima pontificum secures

But not from thee thy homely gods ask hecatombs of
>   sheep;
Content are they with what thou giv'st—content with
>   rural crowns;
>   So twine thy humble rosemary wreath,
>   And weave thy fragile myrtle.

The costliest offering softens not the household gods,
>   if wroth,
More surely than a votive cake or grains of crackling
>   salt,
>   Provided that no sin pollute
>   The hands which touch the altar.

Cervice tinget: te nihil attinet
Tentare multa cæde bidentium
   Parvos coronantem marino
     Rore deos fragilique myrto.

Immunis aram si tetigit manus,
Non sumptuosa blandior hostia
   Mollivit aversos Penates
     Farre pio et saliente mica.

ODE XXIV.

ON THE MONEY-SEEKING TENDENCIES OF THE AGE.

This ode, like those with which Book III. commences, appears written with a design to assist Augustus in the task of social reform after the conclusion of the civil

Though, as the lord of treasures which outshine
   The unrifled wealth of Araby and Indus,
The piles on which reposed thy palaces,
   Filled up both oceans, Tuscan and Apulic;*

Yet if dire Fate her nails of adamant
   Into thy loftiest roof-tree once hath driven,†
Thou shalt not banish terror from thy soul,
   Nor from the snares of death thy head deliver.

Happier the Scythians, wont o'er townless wilds
   To shift the wains that are their nomad dwellings;
Or the rude Getæ whose unmeted soil
   Yields its free sheaves and fruits to all in common;§

---

* In reference to the custom of building palaces out into the sea.
   † Si figit adamantinos
      Summis verticibus dira Necessitas
      Clavos."

Various attempts have been made to explain the obscurity of this metaphor. I have adopted Orelli's interpretation, which he considers to be decidedly proved the right one by an Etruscan painting—viz., that while the rich man is busied in casting out the moles and raising the height of his palace, Destiny is seen driving her nails into the top of the building, as if saying to the master, "Hitherto, but no farther; the fated end is come to thyself." Macleane, however, prefers the interpretation of a commentator in Cru-

civil wars. Orelli ascribes the date to A.U.C. 725, 726, Maclcane to 728. It is more purely didactic than the first five odes of this book—that is to say, it has less of the genuine lyrical mode of treating moral subjects. If in that respect inferior to those odes—as regards the higher range of poetry in the abstract—it is inferior to no ode in elevation of sentiment.

CARM. XXIV.

Intactis opulentior
    Thesauris Arabum et divitis Indiæ,
Cæmentis licet occupes
    Tyrrhenum omne tuis et mare Apulicum,*

Si figit adamantinos
    Summis verticibus dira Necessitas
Clavos,† non animum metu,
    Non mortis laqueis expedies caput.

Campestres melius Scythæ,
    Quorum plaustra vagas rite trahunt domos,
Vivunt, et rigidi Getæ,
    Immetata quibus jugera liberas §

quius, who takes "verticibus" for the human head, to most fatal place for a blow. There is no disputing about tastes; but I confess I like this interpretation less than any. Whatever Fate is about to do with her adamantine nails, it seems necessary, for connection with the preceding lines, that she should fix her mark on the ambitious piles which the man is building—not on himself. And if she has driven her nails into his head, she might spare for that head the net or snare to which the poet refers in the line that follows.

§ The habits of the Suevi, as described by Cæsar, Bell. Gall. IV. 1., are here imputed, correctly or not, to the Getæ.

There each man toils but for his single year—
  Rests, and another takes his turn of labour;
There ev'n the step-dame, mild and harmless, gives
  To orphans motherless again the mother.

No dowered she-despot rules her lord, nor trusts
  The wife's protection to the leman's splendour.*
There, is the dower indeed magnificent!
  Ancestral virtue, chastity unbroken,

Shrinking with terror from all love save one;
  Or death the only sentence for dishonour.
Oh, whosoe'er would banish out of Rome
  Intestine rage and fratricidal slaughter,

If he would have on reverent statues graved
  This holy title, "Father of his Country,"
Let him be bold enough to strike at vice,
  Curb what is now indomitable—Licence,

And earn the praise of *after* time! Alas!
  Virtue we hate while seen alive; when vanished,
We seek her—but invidiously; and right
  The virtue dead to wrong some virtue living.

But what avails the verbiage of complaint—
  To rail at guilt, yet punish not the guilty?
What without morals profit empty laws?
  If nor that zone, which, as his own enclosure,

---

* "Nec nitido fidit adultero." Macleane follows Orelli in considering that this means that she does not trust to the influence of the adulterer to protect her from the anger of the husband.

Fruges et Cererem ferunt,
  Nec cultura placet longior annua;
Defunctumque laboribus
  Æquali recreat sorte vicarius.

Illic matre carentibus
  Privignis mulier temperat innocens;
Nec dotata regit virum
  Conjux, nec nitido fidit adultero.*

Dos est magna parentium
  Virtus, et metuens alterius viri
Certo fœdere castitas;
  Et peccare nefas, aut pretium est mori.

O quisquis volet impias
  Cædes et rabiem tollere civicam,
Si quæret PATER URBIUM
  Subscribi statuis, indomitam audeat

Refrenare licentiam,
  Clarus postgenitis; quatenus, heu nefas!
Virtutem incolumem odimus,
  Sublatam ex oculis quærimus invidi.

Quid tristes querimoniæ,
  Si non supplicio culpa reciditur?
Quid leges sine moribus
  Vanæ proficiunt, si neque fervidis

The Sun belts round with fires—nor that whose soil
  Is ice, the hard land bordering upon Boreas—
Scare back the avarice of insatiate trade,
  And oceans are the conquests of the sailor;

If dread to encounter the supreme reproach
  Of poverty, ordains to do and suffer
All things for profit, and desert as bare
  The difficult way that only mounts to virtue?

O were we penitent, indeed, for sins,*
  How we should haste to cast gems, gauds, gold, useless
Save as the raw material of all ill,
  Amid the shouts of multitudes applauding.

Into the vaults of Capitolian Jove;
  Or that safe treasure-house—the nearest ocean!
To weed out avarice dig down to the root,
  And minds relaxed rebrace by rougher training.

Look at yon high-born boy—he cannot ride!
  Horseback too rude for him—the chase too dangerous!
Skilful and brave—to trundle a Greek hoop;
  And break the laws which interdict the dice-box: †

While his mean father with a perjured oath
  Swindles alike his partner and his hearth-guest.
Spurred by one passion—how to scrape the pelf—
  His worthless self bequeaths an heir as worthless.

---

* I adopt the punctuation of Dillenburger and Orelli—viz., that the full stop is at "bene penitet."—See note in Orelli to lines 49, 50.

† "Græco trocho." This hoop, made of metal, was guided by a rod like our hoops nowadays. It seems to have been used in the thoroughfares, and by youths as well as mere children. The

Pars inclusa caloribus
  Mundi, nec Boreæ finitimum latus,
Durataeque solo nives,
  Mercatorem abigunt, horrida callidi

Vincunt æquora navitæ?
  Magnum pauperies opprobrium jubet
Quidvis et facere et pati
  Virtutisque viam deserit arduæ

Vel nos in Capitolium,
  Quo clamor vocat et turba faventium,
Vel nos in mare proximum
  Gemmas et lapides, aurum et inutile,

Summi materiem mali,
  Mittamus, scelerum si bene pœnitet.*
Eradenda cupidinis
  Pravi sunt elementa, et teneræ nimis

Mentes asperioribus
  Formandæ studiis.   Nescit equo rudis
Hærere ingenuus puer,
  Venarique timet; ludere doctior,

Seu Græco jubeas trocho †
  Seu malis vetita legibus alea:
Cum perjura patris fides
  Consortem socium fallat et hospitem,

---

laws against gambling were stringent, and in Cicero's time it was an offence sufficiently serious for Cicero to make it a grave charge against M. Antony that he had pardoned a man condemned for gambling, as he was himself a habitual gambler. Juvenal says that the heir still in his infancy (bullatus) learnt the dice from his father.

The immoderate* riches grow, forsooth, and grow,
   But ne'er in growing can attain completion;
An unknown something, ever absent still,
   Stints into want the unsufficing fortune.

* "Improbae divitiae." "Improbae" has not here the sense of "dishonest" or "iniquitous," as it is commonly translated; it means, rather, "immoderate," "out of all proportion." Macleane

Indignoque pecuniam
   Heredi properet.   Scilicet improbæ
Crescunt divitiæ;* tamen
   Curtæ nescio quid semper abest rei.

rightly observes that "improbus" is one of the most difficult words to which to assign its proper meaning. It implies excess, and that excess must be expressed according to the subject described.

ODE XXV.

HYMN TO BACCHUS.

Of this ode Orelli says, that it belongs more properly than any other ode of Horace to the dithyrambic genus, any closer imitation of which was denied to the language

Whither, full of thee, O Bacchus,
    Am I hurried by thy rapture, with a spirit strange possessed?
Through what forests, through what caverns?
    Underneath what haunted grottoes shall my voice be heard aloud,

Pondering words to lift up Cæsar
    To his rank 'mid starry orders, in the council-halls of Jove?
O for utterance largely sounding,
    Never yet through mouth of poet made the language of the world!

As the slumberless Bacchante
    From the lonely mountain-ridges, stricken still with wonder, sees
Flash the waves of wintry Hebrus,
    Sparkle snows in Thracian lowlands, soar barbarian Rhodopë,

language and taste of the Romans, as savouring of affectation or bombast. Nowhere in Horace is there more of the true lyrical enthusiasm: the picture of the Bacchante, astonished by the landscape stretched below her, is singularly beautiful. Dillenburger and Orelli conjecture the poem to have been written A.U.C. 725-726; Macleane thinks it may have been on the announcement of the taking of Alexandria, A.U.C. 724. It was evidently while some new triumph of Cæsar's was fresh in the mind of the poet and of the public.

CARM. XXV.

Quo me, Bacche, rapis tui
   Plenum? quæ nemora aut quos agor in specus
Velox mente nova? quibus
   Antris egregii Cæsaris audiar

Æternum meditans decus
   Stellis inserere et consilio Jovis?
Dicam insigne, recens, adhuc
   Indictum ore alio. Non secus in jugis

Exsomnis stupet Evias
   Hebrum prospiciens, et nive candidam
Thracen, ac pede barbaro
   Lustratam Rhodopen, ut mihi devio

Such my rapture, wandering guideless,[*]
  Now where river-margents open, now where forest-shadows close.
Lord of Naiads, lord of Mænads,
  Who with hands divinely strengthened, from the mountain heave the ash:

Nothing little, nothing lowly,
  Nothing mortal, will I utter! Oh, how perilously sweet
'Tis to follow thee, Lenæus,
  Thee the god who wreathes his temples with the vine-leaf for his crown!

---

[*] "Ut mihi devio
  Ripas et vacuum nemus
  Mirari libet."

Some of the MSS. have "rupes" instead of "ripas," and that reading is adopted by Lambinus and Muretus. Dillenburger, Orelli, Macleane, and Yonge agree in preferring "ripas," as having the authority of the best MSS. Assuming this latter reading to be right, it renders more appropriate the previous description of the Bacchante's amaze in seeing all the landscape expand before her. The poet then comes on the river-bank as he emerges from the forest, the country thus opening upon him, and again closed in.

Ripas et vacuum nemus
  Mirari libet.* O Naïadum potens
Baccharumque valentium
  Proceras manibus vertere fraxinos:

Nil parvum aut humili modo,
  Nil mortale loquar. Dulce periculum est,
O Lenæe, sequi deum
  Cingentem viridi tempora pampino.

So in Schiller's 'Der Spaziergang' the poet plunges into the wood, and following a winding path, suddenly the veil is rent. The passage is well translated by a lamented friend, Dr Whewell:—

> "Lost is the landscape at once in the dark wood's secret recesses,
>   Where a mysterious path leads up the winding ascent;
>   . . . .
>   Suddenly rent is the veil; all startled, I view with amazement,
>   Through the wood's opening glade, blazing in splendour the day."

I cannot help thinking that Horace had in his mind an actual scene, as Schiller had in the Walk—that it was in some ramble amidst rocks, woods, and water, that the idea of this dithyramb occurred to him. We have his own authority for believing that, like most other poets, he composed a good deal in his rural walks,—"circa nemus uvidique Tiburis ripas operosa parvus Carmina fingo."

ODE XXVI.

TO VENUS.

This ode has been generally supposed to be written when Horace had arrived at a time of life sufficiently advanced

I have lived till of late well approved by the fair,
And have, not without glory, made war in their cause;
   Now the wall on the seft side of Venus* shall guard
      My arms, and the lute which has done with the service.

Here, here, place the flambeaux which lit the night-march;
Here, the bows and the crowbars—dread weapons of siege,†
   Carrying menace of doom to the insolent gates
      Which refused at my conquering approach to surrender.

Regal goddess who reignest o'er Cyprus the blest,
And o'er Memphis, unchilled by the snow-flakes of Thrace,
   Lift on high o'er that arrogant Chloë thy scourge,
      And by one smarting touch fright her into submission.

---

* In the temple of Venus, on the left wall, as being most propitious.—MACLEANE. The left side, as the heart side, is now, in many superstitious practices derived from the ancients, considered the best for divinations connected with the affections. In chiromancy, the left hand is examined in preference to the right, not only for the line of life, but for the lines supposed to prognosticate in affairs of the heart.

advanced to retire from the service of the ladies, and
Malherbe, the French poet, had it in his eye when, at
the age of fifty, he made farewell visits to the fair ones
he had courted till then, and informed them that he
resigned his commission in the armies of Cytherea.
But I think with Macleane that the ode represents
nothing more than a successful gallant's first refusal;
and that to apply it to Horace himself, or to assume,
from the opening, that he was getting into years, and
about to abandon lyrical poetry, is to mistake the character and scope of the ode.

CARM. XXVI.

Vixi puellis nuper idoneus,
Et militavi non sine gloria;
  Nunc arma defunctumque bello
    Barbiton hic paries habebit,

Lævum marinæ qui Veneris* latus
Custodit. Hic, hic ponite lucida
  Funalia, et vectes, et arcus
    Oppositis foribus minaces.†

O quæ beatam, diva, tenes Cyprum, et
Memphin carentem Sithonia nive,
  Regina, sublimi flagello
    Tange Chloën semel arrogantem.

† The torches to light the gallant to the house he went to attack, and the crowbar to burst open her door, are intelligible enough. What is meant by "arcus," "the bows," is by no means so clear. The weapon may be merely symbolical (Cupid's bow and arrows), or it may have been the arbalist or cross-bow, and used to frighten the porter.—See Orelli's note.

ODE XXVII.

TO GALATEA UNDERTAKING A JOURNEY.

We know nothing more of Galatea than the ode tells us, by which she appears to have been a friend of Horace's meditating a journey to Greece. Upon the strength of a line in which he asks her to remember him, an attempt has been actually made to include her in the catalogue of Horace's mistresses; whereas the poem, in the digressive introduction of the glorious
fate

Let the ill omen of the shrilling screech-owl,*
Or pregnant bitch, or vixen newly littered,
Or tawny she-wolf skulked down from Lanuvium†
    Convoy the wicked;

Let the snake break off their intended journey,
If their nags start, when arrow-like he glances
Slant on the road—I, where I love, a cautious
    Provident Augur,

---

* "Parræ recinentis." Macleane observes that it is not determined what this bird "parra" was, or whether it is known in these islands. I venture to call it, as other translators have done, the screech-owl, which is still, in Italy as elsewhere, deemed a bird of bad omen. Orelli treats of the subject in an elaborate note, which, however, decides nothing. Yonge says, "I believe it is the owl."—See his note.

fate which awaited Europa, might much more plausibly be supposed to intimate that some lover or spouse of very high degree was reserved for Galatea at her journey's end. The beautiful picture of Europa's flight and remorse is among the instances of Horace's exquisite adaptation of the dramatic element to lyrical purposes.

CARM. XXVII.

Impios parræ recinentis* omen
Ducat, et prægnans canis, aut ab agro
Rava decurrens lupa Lanuvino,†
    Fetaque vulpes:

Rumpat et serpens iter institutum,
Si per obliquum similis sagittæ
Terruit mannos: ego cui timebo
    Providus auspex,

---

† "Rava decurrens lupa Lanuvino." The wolf runs down from the wooded hills round Lanuvium, because that town was near the Appia Via, leading to Brundusium, where Galatea would embark.—MACLEANE, ORELLI. "Rava lupa." What exact colour "rava" means is only so far clear that Horace applies it both to a lion and a wolf. Orelli says the word is properly applied to the colour of the eye, and is between black and tawny, as in many animals. I do not know what animals he means, but the eye of most wild beasts is a deep orange colour or a slaty blue.

Ere the weird crow, reseeking stagnant marshes,
Predict the rain-storm, will invoke the raven
From the far East, who, as the priestlier croaker,
    Shall overawe him.*

Go where thou mayst, be happy; and remember
Me, Galatea! May no chough's dark shadow
Lose thee a sunbeam, nor one green woodpecker
    Dare to tap leftward.†

But see where quick and quivering with the tempest
Glares sloped Orion. I have known the breakers
In Hadria's gulf; and with what fawning smoothness
    Sins the pale west wind.

To feel the blind tumultuous shock of Auster,
The howl of dark seas lashing shores that tremble—
This we wish only to the wives and children
    Of our worst foemen.

Europa, thus to the fair bull deceiving
Trusted her snowy form; thus, ensnared in
The widths of ocean, eyeing its dread monsters,
    Paled from her courage:

---

* The crow flying back to his pool or marsh indicated bad weather. The raven croaking from the east was an omen of good weather, therefore the poet summons the raven in time to forestall the crow. He calls the raven "*oscinem* corvum." The epithet is technically augural. "*Oscines* aves" were birds which the augurs consulted for their note, as they consulted the birds called "præpetes" for their flight. Perhaps the epithet justifies the slight paraphrase in the last two lines of the stanza in translation.

† "Picus," a woodpecker or heighhould.—ORELLI. "The green woodpecker."—YONGE. A vast deal of erudition has been

Antequam stantes repetat paludes
Imbrium divina avis imminentum,
Oscinem corvum prece suscitabo
    Solis ab ortu.*

Sis licet felix, ubicunque mavis,
Et memor nostri, Galatea, vivas:
Teque nec lævus vetet ire picus,†
    Nec vaga cornix.

Sed vides, quanto trepidet tumultu
Pronus Orion. Ego quid sit ater
Hadriæ, novi, sinus et quid albus
    Peccet Iapyx.

Hostium uxores puerique cæcos
Sentiant motus orientis Austri, et
Æquoris nigri fremitum, et trementes
    Verbere ripas.

Sic et Europe niveum doloso
Credidit tauro latus, et scatentem
Beluis pontum mediasque fraudes
    Palluit audax.

lavished upon the question, why the word "lævus," or "leftward," should signify ill luck as applied to the "picus," when the left was considered lucky by the Romans, though unlucky by the Greeks. It is suggested that the comparison may have arisen from the different practice of the Greeks and Romans in taking note of birds—the former facing the north, the latter the south (see Orelli and Macleane). I believe, however, that it was the tap of the woodpecker, and not his flight, that was unlucky. It is so considered still in Italy, and corresponds to our superstitious fear of the beetle called the death-watch. If, therefore, heard on the left or heart side, it directly menaced life.

She who so lately in the tranquil meadows
Called wild flowers due as coronals to wood-nymphs,
Now beheld only through night's darkling glimmer
    Stars and wild waters.

Once reaching Crete, Isle of the Hundred Cities,
"Father," she cried, o'ercome with shame and sorrow,
"A daughter's name, alas, a daughter's duty
    I have abandoned!

"What have I done? what left?* The crimes of virgins
A single death does not suffice to punish.
Am I awake? have I in truth committed
    Sin, and so vilely?

"Or am I guiltless—duped by a vain phantom
Leading a dream out of the ivory portal?
Could I indeed have left for watery deserts
    Home and the field-flowers?

"O that the bull were to my wrath delivered!
O for a sword to hack his horns, and mangle
The monster now so hated, though so lately—
    Woe is me!—worshipped.

"Shameless, my household gods I have forsaken,
Shameless, I loiter on the road to Orcus!
Would to the gods that I were in the desert
    Strayed among lions!

---

* "Unde quo veni." "'Unde' implies not that she was so distracted that she had forgotten from whence she had come, but what an exchange I have made."—MACLEANE.

Nuper in pratis studiosa florum, et
Debitæ Nymphis opifex coronæ,
Nocte sublustri nihil astra præter
    Vidit et undas.

Quæ simul centum tetigit potentem
Oppidis Creten: 'Pater, O relictum
Filiæ nomen pietasque,' dixit,
    Victa furore!

'Unde quo veni?* Levis una mors est
Virginum culpæ. Vigilansne ploro
Turpe commissum, an vitiis carentem
    Ludit imago

Vana, quæ porta fugiens eburna
Somnium ducit? Meliusne fluctus
Ire per longos fuit, an recentes
    Carpere flores?

Si quis infamem mihi nunc juvencum
Dedat iratæ, lacerare ferro et
Frangere enitar modo multum amati
    Cornua monstri.

Impudens liqui patrios Penates;
Impudens Orcum moror. O deorum
Si quis hæc audis, utinam inter errem
    Nuda leones!

"While in these cheeks the bloom be yet unwithered,
And all the sap of the luxuriant life-blood
Make their prey tempting, may this fatal beauty
    Feast the fierce tigers.

"I hear my absent father, 'Vile Europa
Why pause to die? More ways than one, O coward!
Here, at this elm-tree, strangled by thy girdle,
    Sole friend not cast off;

"'Or there, down yonder precipice, plunge headlong
Whirled by the storm-blast to thy grave in ocean;
Unless, O royal-born, it please thee better,
    Sold into bondage,

"'To card the wool of some barbarian mistress,
And share with her the base love of a savage.'"
While thus she raved despairing, Venus softly
    Neared her, arch-smiling,

With the boy-archer—but his bow was loosened;
And sating first her mirth, thus spoke the goddess:
"Thou wilt not scold when this loathed bull returning,
    Yields to thy mercy.

"Know thyself bride of Jove the all-subduing.
Hush sobs; learn well to bear thy glorious fortune;
Thou on one section of the globe* bestowest
    Name everlasting."

---

* "Sectus orbis" literally means "half the world," as the ancients divided our planet only into the two great divisions, Europe and Asia.

Antequam turpis macies decentes
Occupet malas, teneræque succus
Defluat prædæ, speciosa quæro
   Pascere tigres.

"Vilis Europe," pater urget absens:
"Quid mori cessas? Potes hac ab orno
Pendulum zona bene te secuta
   Lædere collum.

Sive te rupes et acuta leto
Saxa delectant, age te procellæ
Crede veloci, nisi herile mavis
   Carpere pensum,

Regius sanguis, domineque tradi
Barbare pellex." Aderat querenti
Perfidum ridens Venus, et remisso
   Filius arcu.

Mox, ubi lusit satis: 'Abstineto,
Dixit, 'irarum calidæque rixæ,
Cum tibi invisus laceranda reddet
   Cornua taurus.

Uxor invicti Jovis esse nescis:
Mitte singultus, bene ferre magnam
Disce fortunam; tua sectus orbis*
   Nomina ducet.'

ODE XXVIII.

ON THE FEAST-DAY OF NEPTUNE.

It is but a waste of ingenious trifling to conjecture who or what Lyde was, or, indeed, if any Lyde whatever

What, on the feast-day of Neptune,
    Can I do better? Up, Lyde! Out from its hiding-place, quick,
Drag forth the Cæcuban hoarded;
    Make an attack upon Wisdom! On to the siege of her fort!

See how the noon is declining,
    Yet, as if day were at stand-still, laggard, thou leav'st in the store
The cask which has lazily slumbered
    Since Bibulus acted as consul; now is its time to awake.

Sing we, by turns, of King Neptune,
    And the green locks of the Nereids; then to thy bow-shapen lyre
Chant us a hymn to Latona,
    And to the swift-footed Dian, and to her arrows of light;

Then, as the crown of thy verses,
    Chant to the goddess who visits, borne on her car by the swans,
Cyclades, Cnidos, and Paphos;
    Night, too, shall have her deserts, and lulabies rock her to sleep.*

whatever existed elsewhere than in the poet's fancy. The poem is very lively and graceful, and evidently intended for general popularity as a song, without any personal application to the writer.

CARM. XXVIII.

Festo quid potius die
　Neptuni faciam? Prome reconditum,
Lyde strenua, Cæcubum,
　Munitæque adhibe vim sapientiæ.

Inclinare meridiem
　Sentis; ac, veluti stet volucris dies,
Parcis deripere horreo
　Cessantem Bibuli Consulis amphoram.

Nos cantabimus invicem
　Neptunum, et virides Nereïdum comas;
Tu curva recines lyra
　Latonam, et celeris spicula Cynthiæ:

Summo carmine, quæ Cnidon
　Fulgentesque tenet Cycladas et Paphon
Junctis visit oloribus;
　Dicetur merita Nox quoque nenia.*

---

* "Dicetur merita Nox quoque nenia." The word "nenia" is applied to funereal dirges, and also, as Dillenburger observes, to the songs by which nurses rocked infants to sleep; and Orelli and Macleane suggest that such is the meaning of the word here.

ODE XXIX.

INVITATION TO MÆCENAS.

No ode of Horace specially addressed to Mæcenas exceeds this in dignity of sentiment and sustained beauty of treatment. Horace's descriptions of summer are always charming, and though he rejects the prosaic minuteness by which modern poets, when describing external nature, make an inventory of scenic details as tediously careful as if they were cataloguing articles for auction, he succeeds in bringing a complete picture before the eye, and elevates the subject of still life by the grace of the figures he places, whether in the fore or

Long since, Mæcenas sprung from Tuscan kings,
A vintage mellowing in its virgin cask,
  Balms to anoint the hair,
    And roses meet for wreaths on honoured brows,

Wait at my home for thee. Snatch leisure brief,
And turn thy gaze from Tibur's waterfalls[*]
  The slopes of Æsula,[†]
    And parricidal Telegon's blue hills;

---

[*] "Ne semper udum Tibur." I interpret "udum" as referring to the cascades of Anio; it may mean the rills meandering through the orchards of Tibur.

[†] Munro has Æfulæ. "The *f* is found in some of the best MSS. of Horace, in the best of the scholiasts, as well as of Livy,

or the back ground. But he has seldom surpassed the beautiful image of summer in its sultry glow and in its languid repose which adorns this ode, in contrast with the statesman, intent on public cares, and gazing on Rome and the hills beyond from his lofty tower. It is unnecessary to point out the nobleness of the comparison between the course of the river and the mutability of human affairs, or the simple grandeur of the lines on Fortune so finely, though so loosely, paraphrased by Dryden; and so applicable to public men that it has furnished with illustrations appropriate to themselves some of the greatest of English statesmen.

Carm. XXIX.

Tyrrhena regum progenies, tibi
Non ante verso lene merum cado,
    Cum flore, Mæcenas, rosarum, et
      Pressa tuis balanus capillis

Jamdudum apud me est. Eripe te moræ;
Ne semper udum Tibur,* et Æsulæ†
    Declive contempleris arvum, et
      Telegoni juga parricidæ.

as shown by Huebner in the Hermes, I. p. 426, who completes the proof by citing three inscriptions, one of them Greek, in which the gentile names, Aefolanus, Aefulanus, Αἰϛουλανός, occur."— Munro's Horace, Introd. XXVIII.

Desert fastidious wealth, and that proud pile
Soaring aloft, the neighbour of the clouds; *
   Cease to admire the smoke,
      The riches, and the roar of prosperous Rome.

Sweet to the wealthy the relief of change;
Nor needs it tapestried woof nor Tyrian pall
   For simple feast, whose mirth
      In humble roofs unknits the brows of Care.

Now, hidden long, Andromeda's bright sire
Glares forth revealed: now rages Procyon,
   And the mad Lion-star, †
      As Sol brings back the sultry days of drought.

Now doth the shepherd, with his languid flock,
Seek streams and shades, and thickets dense, the lair
   Of the rough Forest-God;
      And silent margins miss the wandering winds.

All rest save thou, intent on cares of state
And fears lest aught against thy Rome be planned
   In farthest east, or realm
      Of Persian Cyrus, or by factious Don.

The issues of the Future a wise God
Veils in the dark impenetrable Night,
   And smiles if mortals stretch
      Care beyond bounds to mortal minds assigned.

---

* The lofty tower or belvidere of the palace built by Mæcenas on the Esquiline Hill, whence Nero looked down on the conflagration of Rome.

† This fixes the season to the beginning of July, when Cepheus,

BOOK III.—ODE XXIX.

Fastidiosam desere copiam et
Molem propinquam nubibus arduis;*
   Omitte mirari beatæ
     Fumum et opes strepitumque Romæ.

Plerumque gratæ divitibus vices,
Mundæque parvo sub lare pauperum
   Cœnæ, sine aulæis et ostro,
     Sollicitam explicuere frontem.

Jam clarus occultum Andromedæ pater
Ostendit ignem; jam Procyon furit,
   Et stella vesani Leonis,†
     Sole dies referente siccos:

Jam pastor umbras cum grege languido
Rivumque fessus quærit, et horridi
   Dumeta Silvani; caretque
     Ripa vagis taciturna ventis.

Tu civitatem quis deceat status
Curas, et Urbi sollicitus times,
   Quid Seres et regnata Cyro
     Bactra parent Tanaisque discors.

Prudens futuri temporis exitum
Caliginosa nocte premit deus,
   Ridetque, si mortalis ultra
     Fas trepidat. Quod adest memento

a northern star below Ursa Minor, rises. Cepheus was mythically King of Æthiopia, and father of Andromeda. Procyon rises about the same time, and is followed, eleven days afterwards, by Sirius. Leo completes the picture of summer heat.

That which is present heed, and justly weigh;
All else flows onward as the river runs—
   Now, in mid-channel calm,*
      Peacefully gliding to Etruscan seas;

Now, when wild torrents chafe its quiet streams,
Rolling, along with its resistless rush,
   Loosed crags, uprooted trees,
      And herds and flocks, and the lost homes of men,

While neighbouring forests, and far mountain-peaks
Mingle their roar. Happy † indeed is he,
   Lord of himself, to whom
      'Tis given to say, as each day ends, "I have lived:"

To-morrow let the Sire invest the heaven
With darkest cloud or "purest ray serene,"
   He mars not what has been,
      Nor from Time's sum blots out one fleeted hour.

Fortune, exulting in her cruel task—
Consistent in her inconsistent sport—
   Shifts favours to and fro,
      Now to myself, now to another kind.

---

* Orelli has "æquore"—most of the MSS. "alveo,"—which last reading is adopted by Ritter, Yonge, and Munro.
        † "Cui licet in diem
     Dixisse Vixi."
See Orelli's note against the usual interpretation of this passage. The

Componere æquus; cetera fluminis
Ritu feruntur, nunc medio alveo*
  Cum pace delabentis Etruscum
    In mare, nunc lapides adesos

Stirpesque raptas, et pecus et domos
Volventis una, non sine montium
  Clamore vicinæque silvæ,
    Cum fera diluvies quietos

Irritat amnes. Ille potens sui
Lætusque deget, cui licet in diem
  Dixisse Vixi:† cras vel atra
    Nube polum Pater occupato,

Vel sole puro; non tamen irritum
Quodcunque retro est, efficiet, neque
  Diffinget infectumque reddet,
    Quod fugiens semel hora vexit.

Fortuna sævo læta negotio, et
Ludum insolentem ludere pertinax,
  Transmutat incertos honores,
    Nunc mihi, nunc alii benigna.

---

meaning is,—"Happy the man who at the end of each day can say, 'I have lived.'" Ritter connects "vixi" with all the lines that follow to the end of the ode—a construction which, I suspect, few critics will be inclined to favour.

I praise her seated by me;* if she shake
Her parting wings I give back what she gave,
   And, in my virtue wrapped,
     Make honest Poverty my dowerless bride.

'Tis not for me, when groans the mast beneath
Fierce Africus, to gasp out piteous prayers,
   And bargain with the gods,
     Lest gainful bales from Cyprus or from Tyre

Add to the treasures of the greedy deep;
Then from the wreck my slender boat† the gale
   And the Twin star shall speed,
     Safe with one rower through Ægæan storms.

---

* "Laudo manentem." Orelli says that there is extant a rare coin of the time of Commodus, inscribed "Fortunæ Manenti," in which a woman is represented *seated* holding a horse by the halter

BOOK III.—ODE XXIX.

Laudo manentem;* si celeres quatit
Pennas, resigno quæ dedit, et mea
  Virtute me involvo probamque
    Pauperiem sine dote quæro.

Non est meum, si mugiat Africis
Malus procellis, ad miseras preces.
  Decurrere; et votis pacisci,
    Ne Cypriæ Tyriæque merces

Addant avaro divitias mari:
Tunc me, biremis præsidio scaphæ†
  Tutum, per Ægæos tumultus
    Aura feret geminusque Pollux.

---

with her right hand—in her left a cornucopia. I have availed myself of this image in translating "manentem."

† "Biremis scaphæ," a two-oared boat, rowed by a single rower.—ORELLI.

ODE XXX.

PREDICTION OF HIS OWN FUTURE TIME.

This ode appears clearly intended to be the completing poem of some considerable collection of lyrical pieces, forming in themselves an integral representation of the idiosyncrasies of the poet in character and in genius, thus becoming his memorial or "monumentum." It is therefore generally regarded as the epilogue, not to the Third Book only, but to all the first three books; after the publication of which, Horace made a considerable pause before he published the Fourth. There is a great difference in tone between this and Ode xx. Book II., addressed to Mæcenas. That ode, half sportive, half earnest, seems written in the effer-
vescence

I have built a monument than bronze more lasting,
    Soaring more high than regal pyramids,
Which nor the stealthy gnawing of the rain-drop,
    Nor the vain rush of Boreas shall destroy;
Nor shall it pass away with the unnumbered
    Series of ages and the flight of time.
I shall not wholly die! From Libitina *
    A part, yea, much, of mine own self escapes.
Renewing bloom from praise in after ages,
    My growth through time shall be to fresher youth,
Long as the High Priest, with the Silent Virgin,
    Ascends the sacred Capitol of Rome. †

---

* Venus Libitina, the Funereal Venus—Death.

† Viz., "while the Pontifex Maximus shall, on the ides of every month, go up to the Capitol to offer sacrifices to Vesta, her

BOOK III.—ODE XXX.   115

vescence of animal spirits, and might have been called forth in any moment of brilliant success. But this is written in dignified and serious confidence in the firm establishment of the poet's fame. It is unnecessary to defend Horace here from the charge of vainglory, to which a modern poet, arrogating to himself the immortality of fame, would be exposed. The manners of an age decide the taste of an age. The heathen poets spoke of the immortality of their verses with as little scruple as Christian poets speak of the immortality of their souls. Not to mention the Greek poets, Dillenburger gives a tolerably long list of passages from the Latin—Ennius, Virgil, Propertius, Ovid, Martial—who spoke of their conquest over time with no less confidence than Horace here does. The metre in the original is the same as that of Ode I. Book I., which perhaps strengthens the supposition that the poem is designed to complete a collection which that ode commenced.

CARM. XXX.

Exegi monumentum ære perennius,
Regalique situ pyramidum altius;
Quod non imber edax, non Aquilo impotens
Possit diruere, aut innumerabilis
Annorum series et fuga temporum.
Non omnis moriar, multaque pars mei
Vitabit Libitinam.* Usque ego postera
Crescam laude recens, dum Capitolium †

virgins walking solemnly in the procession, as they did, while the boys sang hymns in honour of the goddess. With a Roman this was equivalent to saying 'for ever.'"—MACLEANE.

From mean estate exalted into greatness—
   Where brawls* loud Aufidus with violent wave,
And arid † reigned o'er rustic subjects, Daunus—
   I, in the lips of men a household name,
Shall have my record as the first who wedded
   To Roman melodies Æolian song.
Take airs of state—the right is earned—and crown me,
   Willing Melpomene, with Delphic bay.

      * "Mantua Virgilio gaudet, Verona Catullo,
        Pelignæ dicar gloria gentis ego."
              —OVID, Amores, III. 15, 17.

Scandet cum tacita Virgine pontifex.
Dicar," qua violens obstrepit Aufidus,
Et qua pauper aquæ Daunus † agrestium
Regnavit populorum, ex humili potens,
Princeps Æolium carmen ad Italos
Deduxisse modos. Sume superbiam
Quæsitam meritis, et mihi Delphica
Lauro cinge volens, Melpomene, comam.

† "Pauper aquæ Daunus," "Daunus scant of water." The epithet is thus, by poetic licence, applied to the legendary king, which, in plain prose, belongs to the country he ruled—*i.e.*, the southern part of Apulia, as the Aufidus flowed through the western

THE SECULAR HYMN.

Religious games, called Ludi Tarentini, Terentini, or Taurii, had been held in Rome from an early period of the Republic. Their origin is variously stated, though the most probable mythical accounts agree that they were instituted and devoted to Dis and Proserpina in consequence of a fearful plague—whether by one Valerius in gratitude for the recovery of his three children, or in the reign of Tarquinius Superbus in order to propitiate those formidable deities. In the latter case the plague had affected pregnant women, and their children died in the womb; and sterile cows (Taureæ) being sacrificed, the games were called Ludi Taurii. By these accounts it would seem that the games were connected with the health of offspring, and by all accounts that they were instituted in honour of Dis and Proserpina. To those eminent scholars who hold to the Etrurian origin of the Tarquins, "the Tarenti and Taurii are but as different forms of the same word, and of the same root as Tarquinius" (Smith's Dict., art. "Ludi Sæculares"). If so, the deities honoured were doubtless Etrurian—not Greek nor Roman—though the Romans subsequently identified them with divinities familiar to their own worship.

Be that as it may, during the Republic these games appear to have been only celebrated three times, at irregular intervals in no way connected with fixed periods or cycles (sæcula).

When Augustus had completed (A.U.C. 737) the second lustre, or the ten years for which the imperial power was first confided to him, it was very natural that he should wish for the solemnity of an extraordinary festival at once popular and religious, and probably also the desire of establishing a dynasty would give rise to the idea of rendering this solemnity regular, but at far-distant dates; thus associating indirectly the duration of the Empire with the welfare and existence of Rome. The custodiers of the Sibylline books, who had been increased from two to ten, and subsequently, probably by Sulla, to fifteen (quindecimviri), were ordered to consult those oracles, and they reported that the time was come to revive the old Tarentine games. They introduced, however, certain innovations, such as the cyclical or secular period, for their celebration (pretending that such periods had been always observed, or at least enjoined), and the substitution of Apollo and Diana for Dis and Proserpina. The latter change seems natural enough. Diana had among her attributes those of Proserpina, and Apollo was the deity whom Augustus especially honoured as his patron god. Dis and Proserpina were no longer in fashion, and were probably never very popular with the genuine Romans; while, as the festival was not designed, like the old Tarentine games, for the averting of some national calamity or mortal disease, but rather to attest the blessings enjoyed under the Empire, and implore their continuance, the direct invocation of the infernal divinities would have been very inappropriate; and, indeed, their powers as averters of evil had become transferred to Apollo and Diana (as the sun and moon), who were also the bestowers of good. Sacrifices were, however, offered to Dis and Proserpina on the first day of the ceremony among other gods, in the list of whom they are placed last. Still it may be seen in the following Hymn that much of the original character of the Tarentine or Taurian games was retained, however modified to suit altered circumstances. Diana is especially implored to protect mothers and mature their offspring. Augustus approaches the altar with white steers for sacrifice, as cows had been sacrificed to Dis in the Taurian games (though, as black animals had been offered to the infernal deities in time of calamity, the white colour of the steers was significant of the change to celestial divinities and the felicity of the period), and the games commenced in the Tarentum—*i. e.*, the same ground that had been consecrated to the Tarentine games. The nature and order of the ceremonies, which lasted three days and three nights, was intrusted to Ateius Capito, a celebrated jurist and antiquary, and Horace was requested to compose the principal hymn on the occasion. The games were held in the summer of the year B.C. 17. They were repeated four times during the Empire, but not at the periods enjoined by the Quindecimviri under Augustus —viz., in cycles of 110 years. The second took place, A.D. 47, in the reign of Claudius; the third, A.D. 88, in the reign of Domitian; and the fourth in the reign of Philippus, A.D. 248. For further particulars of the ceremony the general reader is referred to Smith's Dict., art. "Ludi Sæculares"; and for the mystical belief that the world was moving in a cycle, the completion of which constituted the Magnus Annus, when all the heavenly bodies returned to their original relative places, see Orelli and Macleane's introduction to the

Secular Hymn. As the length of the ten sæcula which constituted the great Platonic year of the universe was not defined, but declared from time to time by prodigies from heaven, so this belief may account for the irregular periods in which the Secular Festival was held during the Empire.

When Horace boasts (Lib. III. Carm. xxx.) that he shall be spoken of as the first who adapted Æolian song to Italian measures, he must mean something more than the mere introduction of Greek lyrical metres into the Italian language. In this task Catullus had preceded him. He nowhere mentions Catullus; and though that omission has been ascribed to jealousy, there is no evidence of so envious a defect in Horace's general character. He bestows lavish praise on the eminent poets of his own time; and a jealous poet is more apt to be jealous of living contemporaries than of defunct predecessors. Nor is it to be forgotten that, if Horace confines his boast to the mere introduction of Lesbian metres, the Sapphics of Catullus must have been sufficiently fresh in popular recollection to afford his enemies one of those opportunities for confuting a boast and turning it into ridicule which are not voluntarily courted by a man of such good sense and of such knowledge of the world as Horace is allowed to have been. And it is not to the Alcaic metre, but exclusively to the Sapphic, as connected with his name, that he refers, Lib. IV. Carm. vi.

> "Ego dis amicum,
> Sæculo festas referente luces,
> Reddidi carmen, docilis modorum
> Vatis Horati."

Horace's boast, then, is only to be justified by the supposition that although Catullus had preceded him in the adoption of the Sapphic metre, he had not adapted it to song—had not incorporated it in the popular form of lyrical music—and Horace had done so, and been the first to do it.

I apprehend, therefore, that Horace's vaunted originality consisted in being the first by whom the borrowed metres were set to Italian music—the first by whom, through arts not before divulged, the words were to be united with musical strings ("Non ante volgatas per artes Verba loquor socianda chordis"— Lib. IV. Carm. ix.), and thus popularised in banquet-halls and temples as national songs (Lib. III. Carm. xi.) It seems to me that in this sense he says he is pointed out as "Romanæ fidicen lyræ" (Lib. IV. Carm. iii.), "fidicen" being a word especially applicable to a musician, and only metaphorically to a poet.

That several of the odes were not adapted to singing does not invalidate this supposition. Such will be the case with every copious lyrical poet, who may, nevertheless, like Moore, have achieved his main popularity through the adaptation of his verse to musical accompaniment and national airs.

Whether the music to which the measures employed by Horace were set was composed by himself in whole or in part, or by others, is a question on which there are no data for legitimate conjecture. If by himself, one might suppose that some record of the fact would be preserved by Suetonius or the scholiasts. On the other hand, if composed by another, it seems strange that a poet of character so grateful as Horace's should have refrained from all mention of one to whom he was under no mean obligations for the popularity his verses had acquired, and with whom he must have

THE SECULAR HYMN. 123

been necessarily brought into frequent and familiar intercourse. It may, however, be said, as sufficient reason for such silence in either case, that a Roman of Horace's day would not have held the art of a musical composer in high account.

The writers who have sought to elucidate the obscure subject of ancient music consider it probable that nothing like the modern system of musical rhythm existed among the ancients, and that, since there is no mention of *notation* distinct from the metre of the song, the time was marked by that metre where vocal music was united with instrumental (Burney's 'History of Music;' Hawkins's 'Hist. of Music;' Smith's Dict., art. "Musica"). By this the reader can judge for himself whether Horace's task in timing the music to his own rhythms would not have been comparatively easy; and whether, if it were thus easy, it would have been considered worthy of commemoration by his contemporaries, or been preserved in such brief records of his life as were consulted by Suetonius, or known to the scholiasts.

At all events, Horace appears, on the occasion of the Secular Hymn, to have superintended the rehearsal of the recitative as "διδάσκαλος," according to the custom of dramatic and lyric poets of Greece; and (Lib. IV. Carm. VI.) the young girls who take part in the chorus are enjoined not only to preserve the Lesbian metre, in which the hymn was composed, but to remember "pollicis ictum," the beat of his finger in marking time.

Regarded only as a poem, the Secular Hymn, though it deserves higher praise than Macleane and other critics have bestowed on it, cannot be said to equal the genius exhibited in many of the odes, especially in Book III. But if set—whether by Horace himself, or by others whom he more or less schooled and directed—to some music which became a grand national air, such as 'God save the King,' or 'The Marseillaise,' we can readily account for the special pride with which he refers to it, and the increased rank which it appears to have won for him in popular estimation.

In

O Phœbus, and O forest-queen Diana,
Ye the twin lustrous ornament of heaven,
Though ever holy, in this time most hallowed
    Be most benign to prayer!

For duly now, as Sibyl verse enjoins us,
Pure youths, with chosen virgins linked in chorus,
To Powers divine o'er the Seven Hills presiding,
    Uplift the solemn hymn.

O Sun, the nurturer,* in bright chariot leading
Day into light to hide it under shadow,
Born still the same, yet other, mayst thou never
    See aught more great than Rome!

Blest Ilithyia, † mild to watch o'er mothers,
And aid the timely coming of the new-born,
Whether thou rather wouldst be as Lucina
    Or Genitalis hailed,

---

* "Alme Sol." This epithet is to be taken in its proper sense as derived from *alo*, Sun the Nurturer.—MACLEANE.

† "Ilithyia." This name, here applied to Diana, is equally applicable to Juno, and, in the plural number, to the minor deities attending on childbirth. There appears to me, if I mistake not, a singular beauty which has escaped the commentators in the choice of names here given to Diana. Ilithyia and Lucina (the one

In the Secular Hymn, and in some of the Sapphic odes of the Fourth Book, Horace more conforms than he does in the first three books to the Greek usage, in the variation of the cæsura and the introduction of the trochee in the second place. I have judged it necessary, for the solemnity of feeling which is instilled into this poem, to add another foot to the fourth line in the translation.

CARM. SÆCULARE.

Phœbe, silvarumque potens Diana,
Lucidum cæli decus, O colendi
Semper et culti, date, quæ precamur
    Tempore sacro;

Quo Sibyllini monuere versus
Virgines lectas puerosque castos
Dis, quibus septem placuere colles,
    Dicere carmen.

Alme Sol,* curru nitido diem qui
Promis et celas, aliusque et idem
Nasceris, possis nihil urbe Roma
    Visere majus.

Rite maturos aperire partus
Lenis, Ilithyia, † tuere matres;
Sive tu Lucina probas vocari,
    Seu Genitalis:

Greek, the other Latin) are names which Diana shares with Juno, and therefore, as applied to childbirth, imply the children born in sacred wedlock. The name "Genitalis" is that which Diana shares with Venus, and therefore implies the offspring of chaste if ardent love. Thus, "whether thou preferrest the name of Lucina or Genitalis," would mean, "whether thou preferrest the name that associates thee with Juno or that which associates thee with Love."

Goddess as each, mature our offspring; prosper
The law that guards the sanctity of marriage,*
And may it give new blossom and new fruitage
    To the grand parent-stem!

So that as each eleventh solennial decade
Round to its close, this sacred feast renewing,
In song and sport, assembled Rome may hallow
    Three days and joyous nights.

And ye, O Parcæ, who have sung prophetic
Truths,† which, once said, the sure events determine,
Fixed as divine decrees,—a glorious future
    Join to the glorious past.

Fertile in fruits and flocks, let Earth maternal
With spikèd corn-wreath crown the brows of Ceres;
Pure from all taint let airs and dews of heaven
    Nourish the new-born life.

Mild, all thine arrows sheathed within the quiver,
Hear thy boy-suppliants, merciful Apollo; §
Hear thy girl-votaries, crescent-crownèd Luna,
    Queen of the clustered stars.

---

* The Julian law (de maritandis ordinibus), for the discouragement of celibacy and the regulation of marriage, was among the social and moral reforms aimed at by Augustus, and passed the year before the celebration of the Secular games. It appears to have been a law well meant, but in some respects singularly unwise and impracticable. The unmarried person could not succeed to a legacy unless he married within a hundred days after the bequest. Fancy poor Horace himself condemned to decide between forfeiting the bequest of a villa at Tarentum or marrying some Glycera or Pyrrha!

Diva, producas sobolem, Patrumque
Prosperes decreta super jugandis
Feminis, prolisque novæ feraci
    Lege marita:*

Certus undenos decies per annos
Orbis ut cantus referatque ludos,
Ter die claro, totiesque grata
    Nocte frequentes.

Vosque veraces cecinisse,† Parcæ,
Quod semel dictum est, stabilisque rerum
Terminus servat, bona jam peractis
    Jungite fata.

Fertilis frugum pecorisque Tellus
Spicea donet Cererem corona;
Nutriant fetus et aquæ salubres,
    Et Jovis auræ.

Condito mitis placidusque telo
Supplices audi pueros, Apollo;§
Siderum regina bicornis, audi,
    Luna, puellas:

---

† Viz., the oracular Sibylline verses.

§ This line seems to refer to the new statue of the Apollo of Actium set up by Augustus in the Palatine temple. In the Apollo of Actium invoked by Augustus before his battle with M. Antony, the bow is bent—in the Apollo of the Palatine the bow is laid aside for the lyre and plectrum.—See MACLEANE'S excellent note on this line.

If Rome be your work—if beneath your safeguard
A band of wanderers, Ilion's scanty remnant,
Ordained to change their city and their Lares,
    Have held this Tuscan land—

They, unto whom, through Troy that blazed unharming,
Pure-souled Æneas, his lost land's survivor,
Opened free path, and heritage more ample
    Than aught relinquished gave;

Gods, grant to docile youth worth's upright manners—
Gods, grant to placid age worth's calm contentment—
Grant to the Roman race growth, power, and riches,[*]
    And all that can adorn!

Bless him who nears with milk-white steers your altars,
Whose blood flows bright from Venus and Anchises;
Still every foe in battle may he conquer,
    And after conquest spare.

Awed by our arms, and by the Alban lictors,[†]
Now the Mede owns our power on land and ocean;
Now Ind and Scythia, she of late so haughty,
    To Rome for pardon sue.[§]

Now Faith and Peace, and antique Shame and Honour
Flock fearless back, and Virtue long-neglected;
And with them comes their sure companion Plenty,
    Rich with o'erflowing horn.

---

[*] "Remque prolemque." "Res" seems here used in its double signification of power and riches. The nearest approach to its sense in a single word would perhaps be the old Anglo-Saxon "weal."

[†] Viz., by our military prowess and civil justice.

[§] "Responsa petunt." "Responsa" here has many significations, the choice of which may well baffle a translator. It may mean replies to proffered amity and submission—it may mean the

Roma si vestrum est opus, Iliæque
Litus Etruscum tenuere turmæ,
Jussa pars mutare Lares et urbem
    Sospite cursu;

Cui per ardentem sine fraude Trojam
Castus Æneas patriæ superstes
Liberum munivit iter, daturus
    Plura relictis;

Di, probos mores docili juventæ,
Di, senectuti placidæ quietem,
Romulæ genti date remque* prolemque
    Et decus omne!

Quæque vos bobus veneratur albis
Clarus Anchisæ Venerisque sanguis,
Impetret, bellante prior, jacentem
    Lenis in hostem!

Jam mari terraque manus potentes
Medus, Albanasque timet secures; †
Jam Scythæ responsa § petunt, superbi
    Nuper, et Indi.

Jam Fides, et Pax, et Honos, Pudorque
Priscus, et neglecta redire Virtus
Audet; apparetque beata pleno
    Copia cornu.

---

opinions given by a jurisconsult to his client, or the mandates of the imperial government to its dependants—or it may mean replies to the prayer of the barbarians to be admitted to the protection and equity of the Roman laws, or the responses vouchsafed by an oracular or godlike power to a suppliant for relief or pardon. The last construction is adopted in the translation.

May he adorned with fulgent bow—the Augur,
Phœbus, the darling of the nine Camenæ—
He the mild Healer, lifting the sore burden
    That weighs down weary limbs*—

If shrines in Palatine he views with favour,
The coming lustre bless, and link it onward
To those yet brighter, through all time prolonging
    Rome and the Latian race.

And oh, may She who holds the sacred hill-tops
Of Aventine and Algidus, Diana,
To the Fifteen,† and to her own young vot'ries,
    Lend an approving ear!

So we, the choir of Dian and of Phœbus,
Versed in their praise, take home with us hope certain
That, heard by Jove and each divine Immortal,
    These words are felt in heaven.

---

* Apollo is here addressed in his fourfold capacity: 1stly, As the god of power, but adorned rather than armed (as at Actium) with his bow; 2dly, As the prophetic seer or augur (the religious attribute); 3dly, As the beloved of the Muses—*i.e.*, the patron of peaceful arts and letters; 4thly, As the divine healer, which may, perhaps, here be used in a latent signification, healer of the pains and wounds of the civil wars. Possibly all these attributes may

THE SECULAR HYMN.

Augur, et fulgente decorus arcu
Phœbus, acceptusque novem Camenis,
Qui salutari levat arte fessos
    Corporis artus, *

Si Palatinas videt æquus arces,
Remque Romanam Latiumque felix
Alterum in lustrum, meliusque semper
    Proroget ævum.

Quæque Aventinum tenet Algidumque,
Quindecim Diana preces virorum †
Curet, et votis puerorum amicas
    Applicet aures.

Hæc Jovem sentire, deosque cunctos,
Spem bonam certamque domum reporto,
Doctus et Phœbi chorus et Dianæ
    Dicere laudes.

---

have been symbolised in the pedestal of the statue, or on the walls of the Palatine temple, to which direct reference is made in the following stanza.

† "Quindecim—virorum," the elect Fifteen who had the custody of the Sibyl books, the charge of the Secular games and solemnities, and in fact, were the priesthood of Apollo.—See Smith's Dictionary, art. "Ludi Sæculares."

BOOK IV.—ODE I.

Franke, in his 'Fasti Horatiani,' assumes the first three books of the Odes to have been composed between A.U.C. 724 and 730, in which latter year, or in the beginning of 731, they were given to the public, in the interval between Horace's thirty-eighth and forty-first year. Horace then appears to have devoted himself chiefly to his Epistles, and not to have published the Fourth Book of Odes till A.U.C. 741, when he was in his fifty-second year. It is said that Augustus had expressed a desire for its publication, as comprising the odes (IV. and XIV.) in honour of the victories of Drusus and Tiberius. These two odes are indeed unexcelled,

  Wars long suspended, now
Urgest thou, Venus? Spare! O spare! I pray;
  I am not what I was
Under the reign of good Queen Cinara.

  Mother of loves so sweet,
Thyself so cruel, cease to subject him
  Whom the tenth lustre finds
No longer pliant to thy soft commands:

excelled, even by the finest in the three preceding books; nor are most of the others below the standard of Horace's matured genius. The first ode was, he says himself, written in his fiftieth year. Macleane, in common with some other commentators, conjectures that it may have been an imitation from the Greek, and adds "that he may have published it to fill up his book, not as a prologue to it, as many of the chronologists say,—for what is there in this ode that bears that character?" Not much, indeed, unless Horace wished to apprise his readers that they are not to expect in this book the lighter gallantries which had place in the former books. This book, indeed, only contains two love-poems besides the first—viz., the tenth and the eleventh; and one is glad to think that the tenth (omitted in the translation) was merely an artistic imitation or translation from the Greek.

Carm. I.

Intermissa, Venus, diu
    Rursus bella moves? Parce, precor, precor.
Non sum qualis eram bonæ
    Sub regno Cinaræ. Desine, dulcium

Mater sæva Cupidinum,
    Circa lustra decem flectere mollibus
Jam durum imperiis: abi,
    Quo blandæ juvenum te revocant preces.

Go where, with blandishing prayers,
Youth calls thee back; hearts easier kindled seek,
　And, borne on purple wings,
Greet Paullus Maximus* in banquet hours.

Noble and fair is he;
Nor his the lips to pleading suitors mute;
　Youth of a hundred arts
To bear thy conquering standards wide and far;

Whene'er some rival, rich
In gifts, he conquers, laughing, he shall place,
　By Alban waters, under citron roofs,
Imaged in marble, Thee.

There shalt thou take delight
In spicèd balms, and songs commingled sweet
　With Berecynthian fife
And lyre—nor silent be the fluten reed.

There, twice a-day, shall youths
Choral with tender maidens, chant thy name,
　As thrice, in Salian dance,
Quakes the green sod to feet that twinkle white.

---

* If, as Estré observes ('Horat. Prosop.'), this be the Paullus Fabius Maximus who was consul A. U. C. 743, the words "centum artium puer" could scarcely be applied to him, even in the widest sense in which the poets took the word "puer" or "juvenis." In fact he could not well have been younger than Horace. On the

Tempestivius in domum
  Paulli, purpureis ales oloribus,
Comissabere Maximi,*
  Si torrere jecur quæris idoneum:

Namque et nobilis, et decens,
  Et pro sollicitis non tacitus reis,
Et centum puer artium
  Late signa feret militiæ tuæ:

Et, quandoque potentior
  Largi muneribus riserit æmuli,
Albanos prope te lacus
  Ponet marmoream, sub trabe citrea.

Illic plurima naribus
  Duces thura, lyræque et Berecyntiæ
Delectabere tibiæ
  Mixtis carminibus, non sine fistula.

Illic bis pueri die
  Numen cum teneris virginibus tuum
Laudantes, pede candido
  In morem Salium ter quatient humum.

---

other hand, if, as some commentators, including Ritter, suppose, it was the son of this P. Maximus and the friend of Ovid who is meant, he would, it is true, have only been about twenty; but how could the line "pro sollicitis non tacitus reis," which refers to his eloquence as an advocate, apply to a youth of that age?

But me nor youth nor maid
Allures, nor faith in intermingled souls,
　　Nor to contend in wine;
No vernal flowerets wreathe my temples now.

* * * * *
* * * * *
* * * * *

Me nec femina nec puer
  Jam nec spes animi credula mutui,
Nec certare juvat mero,
  Nec vincire novis tempora floribus.

Sed cur heu, Ligurine, cur
  Manat rara meas lacrima per genas?
Cur facunda parum decoro
  Inter verba cadit lingua silentio?

Nocturnis ego somniis
  Jam captum teneo, jam volucrem sequor
Te per gramina Martii
  Campi, te per aquas, dure, volubiles.

ODE II.

TO IULUS ANTONIUS.

Iulus Antonius was the second son of M. Antony the triumvir by Fulvia; the elder, Antyllus, was put to death by Octavian after the battle of Actium. Iulus, then in his infancy, was brought up with great tenderness by his stepmother Octavia, married her daughter Marcella, and rose to the highest honours of the State —prætor, A.U.C. 741; consul, A.U.C. 744. His end was tragical. He was either executed by Augustus or destroyed himself, A.U.C. 752, in the forty-second year of his age, on the charge of adultery with Julia, to which crime he is said to have been induced by ambitious designs on the Empire. Iulus possessed the literary accomplishments for which so many of the Roman nobles in that day were remarkable. He was a pupil of L. Crassitius, a celebrated grammarian, at whose school were instructed youths of the first Roman families. According to the scholiasts, he composed not only works in prose, but twelve books in heroic verse upon Diomed, which Acron styles "egregios;" though, as Macleane observes with his customary good sense, "As it is most likely Acron never saw them, his testimony

Iulus, he who would with Pindar vie,
Soars, with Dædalian art, on waxen wings
And falling, gives his name unto the bright
    Deeps of an ocean.*

---

* As Icarus gave his name to the Icarian sea.

testimony is not worth much." Horace, however, in this ode pays a high compliment to his poetic powers. The ode itself is a noble homage to Pindar, and interesting for Horace's estimate of his own peculiar powers, and his frank confession of the pains he took with his verses. The poem was written during Augustus's absence from Rome for two years, when, A.U.C. 737, the Sygambri, a fierce German tribe (whose name Jac. Grimm derives from "sigu," victory, and "gomber," strong), had, with two other tribes, invaded the Roman territory in Gaul, and defeated the Roman legate Lollius with great slaughter. Augustus went in person into Gaul. The German tribes retreated at his approach, gave hostages, and obtained peace. Augustus, however, did not return to Rome till he had restored order in Germany, Gaul, and Spain. As he was expected in Rome long before he returned, the ode was probably written soon after the Sygambri had given hostages and obtained peace, A.U.C. 738, or beginning of 739. It is commonly supposed that Antonius had urged Horace to celebrate the triumphs of Augustus in Pindaric style, and that he modestly excuses himself from that request. The tone of the ode favours this assumption, though it does not leave it clear that Antonius had made such a request.

Carm. II.

Pindarum quisquis studet æmulari,
Iule, ceratis ope Dædalea
Nititur pennis vitreo daturus
    Nomina ponto.*

As from the mountain-top a headlong stream,
Nourished by rains beyond familiar banks,
So seethes, and, measureless with utterance deep,
    Rushes down Pindar.

All due to him Apollo's laureate crown,
Whether through daring dithyrambs he roll
Language new-formed,* borne on the lawless wave
    Of his wild music;

Whether he sing of gods or god-born kings,
By whom the Centaurs with just doom were slain,
And dire Chimæra's flame was quenched; or those
    Palm-crowned in Elis,

Led as Celestials home; and chants the strife
Of steed or cestus; offering gifts, o'er time
More potent than a hundred monuments
    Wrought from the marble;

Or wails the youth snatched from a weeping bride,
And, in lamenting, lifts his force of soul,
Valour, and golden worth, unto the stars,
    Foiling black Orcus.

Ample the gale which buoys the Theban swan,
Oft as he seeks his altitude in clouds.
I, like the bee of the Matinian hill,
    Gather the wild-thyme,

---

* "Nova verba," "new forms of expression."

Monte decurrens velut amnis, imbres
Quem super notas aluere ripas,
Fervet immensusque ruit profundo
    Pindarus ore;

Laurea donandus Apollinari,
Seu per audaces nova dithyrambos
Verba * devolvit numerisque fertur
    Lege solutis;

Seu deos regesve canit, deorum
Sanguinem, per quos, cecidere justa
Morte Centauri, cecidit tremendæ
    Flamma Chimæræ;

Sive quos Elea domum reducit
Palma cælestes, pugilemve equumve
Dicit et centum potiore signis
    Munere donat;

Flebili sponsæ juvenemve raptum
Plorat, et vires animumque moresque
Aureos educit in astra, nigroque
    Invidet Orco.

Multa Dircæum levat aura cycnum,
Tendit, Antoni, quotiens in altos
Nubium tractus. Ego apis Matinæ
    More modoque,

With lavish labour hiving thrifty sweets;
Lowly, by Tibur's grove and dewy banks,
I seek the honey that I store in song,*
    Kneaded with labour.

But thou, the minstrel of a grander lyre,
Celebrate Cæsar, when his laurelled brow
Looks from the car which, up the sacred hill,
    Drags the Sygambri;

He, than whom never to this earth have Fate
And kind gods given, nor shall give, ev'n if yet
The Golden Age come back to mortals, aught
    Better or greater.

Chant thou the games that honour the return
Of brave Augustus granted to our prayer;
The joyous feast-days, the hushed courts of law,
    Vacant of suitors.

Then, too, if aught that I can speak be heard,
My voice shall aid to swell the choral hymn,
And sing "All hail, thou fair auspicious sun,†
    Bringing back Cæsar!"

---

* "Carmina fingo." "Fingo" corresponds to "πλάττω," which word the Greeks used especially with reference to the making of honey.—ORELLI, MACLEANE.

† "Et, O Sol
Pulcher! O laudande! canam, recepto
Cæsare felix."

It is uncertain whether "felix" refers to Horace, as "happy in the

Grata carpentis thyma per laborem
Plurimum circa nemus uvidique
Tiburis ripas operosa parvus
　　Carmina fingo.*

Concines majore poëta plectro
Cæsarem, quandoque trahet feroces
Per sacrum clivum merita decorus
　　Fronde Sygambros,

Quo nihil majus meliusve terris
Fata donavere bonique divi,
Nec dabunt, quamvis redeant in aurum
　　Tempora priscum.

Concines lætosque dies et Urbis
Publicum ludum super impetrato
Fortis Augusti reditu, forumque
　　Litibus orbum.

Tum meæ, si quid loquar audiendum,
Vocis accedet bona pars, et, O Sol
Pulcher! O laudande! canam, recepto
　　Cæsare felix.†

return of Cæsar," or to the sun, forming part of the exclamation; Macleane leaves the choice to the reader's taste; Vossius and others prefer the latter application; Orelli considers the former more tender. To me it seems according to the genius of lyrical composition to apply the epithet to the sun. We know already that Horace is happy in the return of Cæsar, otherwise he would not be joining in the procession and the hymn.

And while, O god of triumph, slowly on*
He moves in state, shout upon shout repeats
"Io Triumphe!" through the length of Rome;
    Frankincense steaming

Up to benignant gods. Ten bulls, ten kine,
Acquit thy vow; a single steerling mine,
Fresh-weaned, and browsing into youth amid
    Prodigal pastures;

His frontal imitates the curvèd gleam
Of the young moon in her third night;—all else
Of tawny colour, on that front of snow
    Shimmers her signet.†

---

* "Teque, dum procedit, io Triumphe," not "tumque dum procedit," as in some of our popular editions. It is the god Triumph which is invoked by "io Triumphe." Orelli prefers "procedit" to "procedis," which has good authority in the MSS. (see his note), and refers it to Augustus: "O god of Triumph; while he, Augustus, proceeds, we," &c. Macleane sees no reason for this preference, and adopts the text of Dillenburger, "procedis," which is also favoured by Ritter and Munro. Yonge follows Orelli.

† The conclusion of the ode has been, plausibly enough, blamed for a discrepancy amounting to bathos between the gravity and ele-

BOOK IV.—ODE II.

Teque, dum procedit, io Triumphe,*
Non semel dicemus, io Triumphe,
Civitas omnis dabimusque divis
    Thura benignis.

Te decem tauri totidemque vaccæ,
Me tener solvet vitulus, relicta
Matre qui largis juvenescit herbis
    In mea vota,

Fronte curvatos imitatus ignes
Tertium Lunæ referentis ortum,
Qua notam duxit, niveus videri,
    Cetera fulvus.†

---

vation of the preceding stanzas, and the familiar details of the steerling to be sacrificed — "Desinit in vitulum mulier formosa superne" (STEINER). Orelli, on the contrary, thinks it conformable to poetic art, that the height of enthusiasm should subside, as it were, in the placid anticipation of the destined sacrifice. Possibly Horace meant also, in describing the animal so minutely as already reserved for the sacrifice, to imply how eagerly expected was the return of Augustus;—the victims were already marked, the preparations already made.

ODE III.

TO MELPOMENE.

The sweetness and dignity of this ode have been a theme of unqualified praise to the critics. It was evidently

Whom thou, Melpomene,
Hast once with still bright aspect marked at birth, *
  On him no Isthmian toils
Shall shed the lustre of an athlete's fame;

Him shall no fiery steed
Ravish to victory in Achaian car;
  In him no warlike deeds
Shall, from the hill-top of the Capitol,†

Show to a world's applause
The glorious image of a conquering chief,
  With Delian leaves adorned,
Who crushed the swelling menaces of kings;

Yet him shall streams that flow
Through fertile Tibur, and the thick-grown locks
  Of the green forest-kings,
Endow with lordship—in Æolian song.

---

* "Nascentem placido lumine videris." The image here is taken from astrology. To Melpomene is ascribed the influence of the planet ascendant at birth, and by which, in technical terms, the "Native" (or new-born) is "aspected."

evidently written after the Secular Hymn, which gave authority and sanction to Horace's claim to be "Romanæ fidicen lyræ."

Carm. III.

Quem tu, Melpomene, semel
    Nascentem placido lumine videris,*
Illum non labor Isthmius
    Clarabit pugilem, non equus impiger

Curru ducet Achaico
    Victorem, neque res bellica Deliis
Ornatum foliis ducem,
    Quod regum tumidas contuderit minas,

Ostendet Capitolio: †
    Sed quæ Tibur aquæ fertile præfluunt,
Et spissæ nemorum comæ,
    Fingent Æolio carmine nobilem.

       † "Neque res bellica Deliis
      Ornatum foliis ducem,
        Quod regum tumidas contuderit minas,
      Ostendet Capitolio."

"Ostendet" is a word borrowed from the ceremonies designed for pomp and ostentation. The victorious general was shown at the Capitol, where he returned thanks to Jove and the gods, deposited the spoils, and received the homage of the world. —Torrentius, Dacier.

Me have the sons of Rome,
Sovereign of cities, deigned to enrol amidst
　The choir beloved of bards;
And now even Envy bites with milder fang.

O thou Pierian Muse,
That tun'st the sweet clash of the golden shell;
　Thou who, if such thy will,
Couldst make mute fishes musical as swans,

Thine is the boon, all thine,
That I am singled from the passers-by,
　"Lyrist of Roman song!"—
Thine that I breathe and please, if please I may.*

---

* "Quod spiro," "that I breathe the breath of song"—"quod movet me spiritus poeticus."—DILLENBURGER, ORELLI, RITTER.

Romæ principis urbium
  Dignatur soboles inter amabiles
Vatum ponere me choros;
  Et jam dente minus mordeor invido.

O testudinis aureæ
  Dulcem quæ strepitum, Pieri, temperas,
O, mutis quoque piscibus
  Donatura cycni, si libeat, sonum,

Totum muneris hoc tui est,
  Quod monstror digito prætereuntium
Romanæ fidicen lyræ:
  Quod spiro et placeo, si placeo, tuum est.*

ODE IV.

IN PRAISE OF DRUSUS AND THE RACE OF THE NEROS.

When, A.U.C. 738-9, Augustus and Tiberius were in Transalpine Gaul, the fierce tribes of the Vindelici and Ræti (the first occupying a considerable range of country between the Danube and Lake Constance, the last neighbouring them to the south, and extending to Lake Como) made forays into Italy and Cisalpine Gaul, attended with great cruelty and massacre. Augustus sent against them Drusus, the younger brother of Tiberius, who was then in his twenty-third year. He defeated and drove them from Italy. It is clearly in honour of the victory under Drusus that the ode is composed. But as these tribes renewed their predatory incursions into Gaul, Tiberius was sent to the aid of Drusus with additional forces. Thus united, the two brothers reduced these and other tribes—such as the Genauni and Breuni—into the Roman province of Rætiæ (Rætia Prima and Secunda). It was in honour of this completed conquest, and of the part which Tiberius had in it, that Ode XIV. was composed, and, as may be reasonably supposed, somewhat subsequently to Ode IV. The opening of this poem is unusually lengthy and involved. It takes four strophes, or sixteen verses,

Even as the thunder's wingèd minister—
To whom, proved true to Jove's entrusted charge
  In gold-haired Ganymede,
    Heaven's king gave kingdom over wandering birds—

verses, before it disentangles itself of its similes, and reaches their application. I do not think that it deserves the blame some critics have attached to it for the slowness and complication with which the image of the young eagle is worked out; perhaps, indeed, the hesitating efforts of the bird before it gathers strength to attack dragons are artistically expressed in the labour of the verse. But I venture to doubt whether the poem would not have been better without the second simile of the lion-whelp, which has no novelty to recommend it, and is very inferior in picturesque vigour to the first one, while it is less appropriate to the eulogy on Drusus. The young eagle training itself to grapple with dragons that resist it, conveys an image of force against force; but it is very little honour to a lion-whelp to conquer a helpless roe-deer or she-goat. "Caprea" means either, but Yonge appears to me right in giving the former interpretation to the word in this passage. Ritter vindicates the simile of the lion-whelp, observing that the illustration of the sheepfold and the dragons would not be appropriate to the Ræti, and that therefore the poet adds the image by which they and Drusus are comprehended.

CARM. IV.

Qualem ministrum fulminis alitem,
Cui rex deorum regnum in aves vagas
   Permisit, expertus fidelem
     Juppiter in Ganymede flavo,

Urged from his eyrie by the goad of youth,
And pulses glowing with ancestral fire,
   Learns from the winds of spring,
     When gone the rain-clouds, timidly to soar,

Till on the sheepfold rushes down its foe;
Next, bolder grown, the hungering greed not less
   Of battle than of food,
     Drives him on dragons that resist his beak;

Or as in gladsome pastures the wild roe,
About to die by fangs unfleshed before,
   Sees the fierce lion-whelp,
     Fresh from the udders of the tawny dam;—

So the Vindelici young Drusus saw
Leading war home to their own Rætian Alps;*
   Whence from all time they learned
     To arm their hands with Amazonian axe†

I pause not now to ask; nor is the lore
Of all things lore allowed; enough that hosts,
   Victorious long and far,
     Vanquished in turn by a young arm and brain,

---

* "Videre Rætis bella sub Alpibus." Macleane agrees with Orelli in adopting Bentley's emendation— "Rætis" instead of "Ræti."—See Orelli's excursus to this ode, and Macleane's comprehensive note. Ritter and Munro have "Ræti."

† "Quibus
Mos unde deductus per omne
Tempus Amazonia securi
Dextras obarmet, quærere distuli:
Nec scire fas est omnia."

These lines are so little in poetic keeping with the noble earnestness

Olim juventas et patrius vigor
Nido laborum propulit inscium:
   Vernique, jam nimbis remotis,
      Insolitos docuere nisus

Venti paventem: mox in ovilia
Demisit hostem vividus impetus:
   Nunc in reluctantes dracones
      Egit amor dapis atque pugnæ:

Qualemve lætis caprea pascuis
Intenta fulvæ matris ab ubere
   Jam lacte depulsum leonem,
      Dente novo peritura vidit:

Videre Rætis bella sub Alpibus*
Drusum gerentem Vindelici; quibus
   Mos unde deductus per omne
      Tempus Amazonia securi†

Dextras obarmet, quærere distuli:
Nec scire fas est omnia; sed diu
   Lateque victrices catervæ,
      Consiliis juvenis revictæ,

of those immediately before and after them, that they have been summarily rejected by several editors, and Franke asserts them to be a silly interpolation. They are, however, justly no doubt, considered genuine by the best of the later authorities. Nor, indeed, are they inconsistent with Horace's habit of introducing a sudden change of playfulness or irony in the midst of his gravest verse. To me they seem evidently a satirical allusion either to some rival poem or to some prosy archæological treatise of his own day upon the origin or customs of the Vindelici; and we lose the point because we have lost the poem or the treatise. Ritter vindicates the digression, and cites in precedent, Pind. Ol. I. 28-42.

Felt what the mind and what the heart achieve,
When reared and fostered amidst blest abodes,
   And with parental love
      A Cæsar's soul inspires a Nero's sons.

Brave and good natures generate natures brave.
In steer and steed ancestral virtue shows.
   Bold eagles never yet,
      Instead of eaglets, begot timorous doves.

Still training speeds the inborn vigour's growth;
Sound culture is the armour of the breast.
   Where fails the moral lore,
      Vice disennobles even the noblest born.

What to the Neros owest thou, O Rome!
Witness Metaurus, routed Hasdrubal,
   And that all-glorious day
      Which chased from Latium the receding shades,

First dawn that laughed with victory, what time
Rode through Italia the dire African,
   As fire through forest-pines,
      Or Eurus over the Sicilian waves.

But from that day, labouring illustrious on,
Victory to victory linked, the Roman grew—
   Till in the shrines laid waste
      By Punic riot and fierce sacrilege,

Once more erect stood forth the gods of Rome.
Then thus outspoke perfidious Hannibal:
   "We deer, foredoomed as prey
      To ravenous wolves, our own destroyers chase,

Sensere, quid mens rite, quid indoles
Nutrita faustis sub penetralibus,
    Posset, quid Augusti paternus
        In pueros animus Nerones.

Fortes creantur fortibus et bonis;
Est in juvencis, est in equis patrum
    Virtus; neque imbellem feroces
        Progenerant aquilæ columbam.

Doctrina sed vim promovet insitam,
Rectique cultus pectora roborant;
    Utcunque defecere mores,
        Indecorant bene nata culpæ.

Quid debeas, O Roma, Neronibus,
Testis Metaurum flumen, et Hasdrubal
    Devictus, et pulcher fugatis
        Ille dies Latio tenebris,

Qui primus alma risit adorea,
Dirus per urbes Afer ut Italas,
    Ceu flamma per tædas, vel Eurus
        Per Siculas equitavit undas.

Post hoc secundis usque laboribus
Romana pubes crevit, et impio
    Vastata Pœnorum tumultu
        Fana deos habuere rectos:

Dixitque tandem perfidus Hannibal:
'Cervi, luporum præda rapacium,
    Sectamur ultro, quos opimus
        Fallere et effugere est triumphus.

"Whom 'tis our amplest triumph to elude,
And, hiding from, escape. Race which, cast forth
  A waif on Tuscan seas
    From Troy's red crater, still had strength to house

"In cities ravished from Ausonian soil,
Its gods, its worship, and its grey-haired sires,
  Yea, and its new-born babes,
    The destined fathers of the men to be;

"Even as the ilex, lopped by axes rude,
Where, rich with dusky boughs, soars Algidus,
  Through loss, through wounds, receives
    New gain, new life—yea, from the very steel:

"Not fiercer did the Hydra hewn, regrow
Against Alcides, chafed to be o'ercome;
  Nor dragon-teeth, earth-sown
    In Thebes or Colchis, spring to armëd men;

"Merged in the deeps, more fair comes forth its star:*
Wrestle and win, it bears the winner down;
  And widowed wives shall tell
    Of victors vanquished on the fields it fought.†

"No more to Carthage shall I send proud news;
Dies, dies the power, the fortune, the renown
  Of the great Punic name;
    Dies hope itself, for Hasdrubal is slain.§

---

* "Evenit." Orelli, following Jahn, has "exiit"—a reading unsanctioned by more recent editors.

† "Prœlia conjugibus loquenda." Orelli considers that the line refers to the Roman wives speaking with exultation of the wars waged by their husbands. Ritter, on the other hand, powerfully supports the interpretation of Mitscherlich—viz., that the line refers to the widows of the slain. His argument seems to me convincing.

Gens, quæ cremato fortis ab Ilio
Jactata Tuscis æquoribus sacra,
   Natosque maturosque patres
      Pertulit Ausonias ad urbes,

Duris ut ilex tonsa bipennibus
Nigræ feraci frondis in Algido,
   Per damna, per cædes, ab ipso
      Ducit opes animumque ferro.

Non Hydra secto corpore firmior
Vinci dolentem crevit in Herculem,
   Monstrumve submisere Colchi
      Majus, Echioniæve Thebæ.

Merses profundo, pulchrior evenit;*
Luctere, multa proruet integrum
   Cum laude victorem, geretque
      Prœlia conjugibus loquenda.†

Carthagini jam non ego nuntios
Mittam superbos: occidit, occidit
   Spes omnis et fortuna nostri
      Nominis, Hasdrubale interempto.§

§ Torrentius considers that here ends the speech attributed to Hannibal, and that in the last verse Horace speaks in his own person—an opinion which has had many followers, and is defended by Ritter. Orelli, supported by Macleane and Yonge, on the other hand, contends that the speech of Hannibal is continued to the close of the ode—firstly, because it is more complimentary to the Neros that their praise and predicted renown should come from the mouth of their foe; secondly, because it is more poetical to conclude the poem with the prophecy of Hannibal, and more in the spirit of Pindar, as Olymp. 4, and Nem. 4. Munro gives his authority to this reading.

"There's nought the hands of men from Claudius sprung
Shall not achieve, with Jove their guardian god,
   Through the sharp stress of war
     Sped by the providence of heedful cares."

Nil Claudiæ non perficient manus;
Quas et benigno numine Jupiter
   Defendit, et curæ sagaces
     Expediunt per acuta belli.'

ODE V.

TO AUGUSTUS, THAT HE WOULD HASTEN HIS RETURN TO ROME.

This ode, which Dillenburger rightly calls "dulcissimum carmen," may be taken in connection with the preceding and with Ode XIV. It was composed during the absence of Augustus in Germany and Gaul, and after the victories of Tiberius and Drusus. Augustus had been absent from September A.U.C. 738 to February 741. In the description of the blessings ascribed to the reign of Augustus, the security to life and

Best guardian of the race of Romulus,
And sprung thyself from deities benign,
Absent too long, fulfil thy promise, pledged
    To Rome's high court*—return.

Bring to thy country back, belovèd chief,
The light: thy looks are to thy people Spring,
And where they smile, more grateful glides the day,
    More genial shines the sun.

As the fond mother with all passionate prayers
Calls back the son more than one year away,
By adverse winds beyond Carpathian seas
    Kept from sweet home afar,

---

* "Sancto concilio"—the Senate.

and property, the reformation of the previous licence of manners,—in short, the change from the calamities of civil war to the felicity of a government firm in maintaining order, and mild enough to be popular beyond all recorded precedent, Horace conveys his own vindication from the charge inconsiderately made against him for his attachment to the empire, and his enthusiasm for the emperor. And however adulatory the language he employs may appear to modern taste, it is no exaggerated expression of the common national sentiment in the times which had exalted Augustus to a share in the honours privately as well as publicly paid to the gods.

CARM. V.

Divis orte bonis, optime Romulæ
Custos gentis, abes jam nimium diu;
Maturum reditum pollicitus Patrum
    Sancto concilio, redi.*

Lucem redde tuæ, dux bone, patriæ:
Instar veris enim voltus ubi tuus
Affulsit populo, gratior it dies,
    Et soles melius nitent.

Ut mater juvenem, quem Notus invido
Flatu Carpathii trans maris æquora
Cunctantem spatio longius annuo
    Dulci distinet a domo,

Fixing intent upon the curving shore
The unmoving stillness of her wistful eyes;—
So for her Cæsar, smit with faithful love,
    His country looks and pines.

Safe* plods the steer among the rural fields;
The rural fields Ceres and Plenty bless;
The winged ships fly through unmolested seas; †
    Honour's fine dread of shame

Returns; no lusts pollute the modest home;
Licence is tamed by manners as by laws; §
Nor reads the husband in his infant's face
    A likeness not his own.

Fast by Crime stands its comrade Punishment.
Who fears the Parthian, who the frozen Scyth?
Who (Cæsar safe) whatever monstrous birth
    Germania's womb conceives?

---

* *I.e.*, under the auspices of Augustus. "Rura perambulat." I adopt Ritter's interpretation that this refers to the ox at the plough, not roving through the pastures. Pales presided over pastures; Ceres, named in the following line, over fields under the plough. The repetition of "rura"—"bos rura perambulat, Nutrit rura Ceres," condemned as a false reading by Bentley and other critics less illustrious, appears to me a peculiar beauty. "Faustitas" is another name for "Copia," "plenty."

† "Pacatum per mare." "Pacatum," "unmolested by pirates." The gratitude of the merchantmen and sailors to Augustus (then Octavian) for putting down piracy is very forcibly expressed in Suetonius, Oct. 98.

§ Horace here refers to the "Lex Julia de Adulteriis," passed by Augustus, A.U.C. 737, and also to an improved standard of na-

Votis ominibusque et precibus vocat,
Curvo nec faciem litore dimovet:
Sic desideriis icta fidelibus
    Quærit patria Cæsarem.

Tutus bos etenim rura perambulat, *
Nutrit rura Ceres, almaque Faustitas,
Pacatum volitant per mare navitæ, †
    Culpari metuit Fides,

Nullis polluitur casta domus stupris,
Mos et lex maculosum edomuit nefas, §
Laudantur simili prole puerperæ,
    Culpam Pœna premit comes.

Quis Parthum paveat? quis gelidum Scythen?
Quis Germania quos horrida parturit
Fetus, incolumi Cæsare? quis feræ
    Bellum curet Hiberiæ?

tional manners. Dion. Cassius (54, 19) implies that one reason for Augustus's expedition to Gaul (that is, absenting himself from Rome) was to get rid of scandal in regard to his alleged intrigue with Terentia, the wife of Mæcenas—which Maclenne rightly dismisses as mere gossip. It is pretty clear, by these verses, either that Horace had heard of no such scandal, or that both he and Mæcenas regarded it with contempt. A poet of so exquisite a taste, and so consummate a knowledge of the world, would not have ventured on the line, "Nullis polluitur casta domus stupris," if such scandal were rife at that very time, or, at least, if any credit were attached to it; for thus the compliment would have been turned into a bitter irony against Augustus, and a cruel insult to Mæcenas.

Let fierce Iberia threaten war—who cares?
Each spends safe days on his own hills, and weds
His vine to widowed elms, then, home regained,
    Brims his glad cup to thee,

Blending with prodigal libation prayers;*
And, as Greece honoured Leda's starry son,
Or great Alcides,—with his household gods
    Mingles thy hallowed name.

Live, O good chief, Rome's feast-days to prolong!
This is our orison at sober morn,
Our prayer with wine-dews on the lip, when sinks
    Underneath seas the sun.

---

* Literally "at his second course;" or rather, as we should say, "at dessert"—"alteris mensis." By a decree of the Senate, libations were to be offered to Octavian after the battle of Actium at private tables as well as in public banquets, and his name to be

Condit quisque diem collibus in suis,
Et vitem viduas ducit ad arbores;
Hinc ad vina redit lætus, et alteris
  Te mensis adhibet deum;*

Te multa prece, te prosequitur mero
Defuso pateris, et Laribus tuum
Miscet numen, uti Græcia Castoris
  Et magni memor Herculis.

Longas, O utinam, dux bone, ferias
Præstes Hesperiæ! dicimus integro
Sicci mane die, dicimus uvidi,
  Cum Sol Oceano subest.

inscribed in hymns of praise as those of the gods.—DION. CASS.,
l. 1-19. It is to these national honours that Horace alludes whenever he speaks of Augustus as enrolled among the gods.

ODE VI.

TO APOLLO.

This ode may be considered the proœmium to the Secular Hymn, A.U.C. 737, although evidently written after it. As that hymn celebrates Apollo and Diana, so this ode appropriately commences with an invocation to Apollo, whom Horace invokes (line 27) to defend

God, in whom Niobe's sad offspring felt
The stern chastiser of the vaunting tongue,
And Tityos vast, the ravisher,—and he,
    Phthian Achilles,

Almost the victor of high Troy (to thee
Unequal, over other force supreme);
Though warring with dread spear the Sea-nymph's son
    Shook Dardan towers,

As falls a pine beneath the biting steel,
Or cypress wrenched by Eurus from its root,
He fell, and wide and far on Trojan dust
    Stamped his great image.

The false horse, duping, in Minerva's name,
Lost Trojans mirthful at their feast of death,
With choral dances blithe in Priam's hall,
    Hid not Achilles.

defend the dignity of the Roman Muse. The poet lingers specially on the praise of Apollo as the slayer of Achilles; because, had he who spared not the babe in the womb survived, Æneas, ancestor of Augustus, and the Trojan exiles who founded the Roman empire, would have perished. Horace, then, after a brief reference to Diana, turns, as choragus, to address the chorus of the Secular Hymn.

CARM. VI.

Dive, quem proles Niobea magnæ
Vindicem linguæ, Tityosque raptor,
Sensit, et Trojæ prope victor altæ
    Phthius Achilles,

Ceteris major, tibi miles impar;
Filius quamvis Thetidis marinæ
Dardanas turres quateret tremenda
    Cuspide pugnax.

Ille, mordaci velut icta ferro
Pinus, aut impulsa cupressus Euro,
Procidit late posuitque collum in
    Pulvere Teucro.

Ille non inclusus equo Minervæ
Sacra mentito male feriatos
Troas et lætam Priami choreis
    Falleret aulam;

His prey, alas! he slew with open hand;
His wrath, alas! had given to Argive flames
The harmless infants even within the womb,
    Smiting the unborn,

Had not the Father of the gods, subdued
By thee and Venus, with imploring prayer,
Pledged to Æneas by his solemn nod
    Walls more auspicious.

Tuneful Thalia's sovereign melodist,
Laving in Xanthian waves thy golden hair,
Support the honour of the Daunian Muse,
    Beardless Agyieus! *

Phœbus on me bestowed the soul, on me
The art of song, on me the poet's name.
† O noblest virgins, and O ye young sons
    Of noble fathers,

Wards of the Delian goddess, with her bow
Striking the flight of stags and lynxes still,
The Lesbian § measure timed and tuned by me,
    Guard unforgetful,

---

* The name of Agyieus seems here very appropriately invoked, because Apollo takes that name from the Greeks, as presiding over the thoroughfares of cities, "quasi viis præpositus urbanis;" and all the streets of Rome would have been alive with the festival and processions connected with the Secular Hymn which the ode refers to.

Sed palam captis gravis, heu nefas! heu!
Nescios fari pueros Achivis
Ureret flammis, etiam latentem
    Matris in alvo;

Ni, tuis victus Venerisque gratæ
Vocibus, divum pater annuisset
Rebus Æneæ potiore ductos
    Alite muros.

Doctor argutæ fidicen Thaliæ,
Phœbe, qui Xantho lavis amne crines,
Dauniæ defende decus Camenæ,
    Levis Agyieu. *

Spiritum Phœbus mihi, Phœbus artem
Carminis, nomenque dedit poëtæ.
Virginum primæ, puerique claris
    Patribus orti, †

Deliæ tutela deæ, fugaces
Lyncas et cervos cohibentis arcu,
Lesbium servate pedem, meique
    Pollicis ictum, §

---

† Here Horace turns to the chorus of the Secular Hymn.
§ "Lesbium servate pedem, meique
    Pollicis ictum."
By "pollicis ictum" is meant the motion of the thumb in marking the rhythm or time of the song, not the striking of the lyre.

Chanting, with ritual due, Latona's son,
And her who kindles night with crescent beam,
Prospers the harvests, and the sliding months
    Speeds in their circle.

Say, maid, then wedded,* "In that hallowed year
Which did the secular feast-lights reillume,
Song dear to gods I sang—song taught by him,
    Horace the poet."

* "Nupta jam dices." Horace here admonishes those who were young virgins in the chorus at the date of the Secular Hymn to remember, when wedded wives, their part in the festival, with which he associates his name.

Rite Latonæ puerum canentes,
Rite crescentem face Noctilucam,
Prosperam frugum, celeremque pronos
    Volvere menses.

Nupta jam dices: * Ego dis amicum,
Sæculo festas referente luces,
Reddidi carmen, docilis modorum
    Vatis Horati.

ODE VII.

TO TORQUATUS.

The Torquatus here addressed appears to be the same Torquatus whom Horace invites to supper, Epist. Lib. I. v. Estré, considering there was no ground for Welchert's assumption that this person was C. Nonius Asprenas Torquatus, mentioned in Suetonius (in Vit. Augusti), expresses his surprise that the commentators had

Fled the snows—now the grass has returned to the meadows,
    And their locks to the trees;
Now the land's face is changed, dwindled rivers receding
    Glide in calm by their shores.

Now, unrobed, may the Grace intertwined with her sisters
    Join the dance of the Nymphs.
"Things immortal, hope not!" saith the Year—saith the Moment
    Stealing off this soft day.

Winter thaws, Spring has breathed; quick on Spring tramples Summer,
    And is gone to his grave;
Appled Autumn his fruits will have shed forth, and then
    Dearth and winter once more.

had not thought of Aulus Torquatus, of whom Nepos speaks in his Life of Atticus, c. 11, who had served with Brutus and Cassius at Philippi, and was therefore Horace's old fellow-soldier. Macleane considers the poem to be one of Horace's earlier odes, and introduced to swell the fasciculus—or, as we should say, fill up the volume. I do not see much cause for that supposition. The sentiment is one habitual to Horace at every stage of his life, and it is in harmony with the tone of the epistle, published probably five or six years before the Fourth Book of Odes.

Carm. VII.

Diffugere nives: redeunt jam gramina campis
 Arboribusque comæ;
Mutat terra vices et decrescentia ripas
 Flumina prætereunt;

Gratia cum Nymphis geminisque sororibus audet
 Ducere nuda choros.
Immortalia ne speres, monet Annus et almum
 Quæ rapit Hora diem.

Frigora mitescunt Zephyris, Ver proterit Æstas
 Interitura, simul
Pomifer Auctumnus fruges effuderit, et mox
 Bruma recurrit iners.

But the swift moons* restore change and loss in the
    heavens,
  When we go where have gone
Sire Æneas, and Tullus,** and opulent Ancus,
  We are dust and a shade.†

Who knows if the gods will yet add a to-morrow
  To the sum of to-day?
Count as saved from an heir's greedy hands all thou
    givest
  To that friend—thine own self.

When once dead, the resplendent § tribunal of Minos
  Having once pronounced doom,
Noble birth, suasive tongue, moral worth, O Torquatus,
  Reinstate thee no more.

Her Hippolytus chaste from the midnight of Hades
  Dian's self could not free;
Lethe's chains coiled around his own best-loved Pi-
    rithous,
  Theseus' self could not rend.

---

* "Damna tamen celeres reparant cælestia lunæ." Macleane appears to me right in differing from Orelli, who refers "damna cælestia" to the changes of the moon. "'Tamen' shows that the changes and deteriorations of the weather and seasons are intended, and 'celeres lunæ' are the quick-revolving months"—*i.e.*, without metaphor, time brings back the seasons—time does not bring back us men when we once vanish.

** Ritter has "Tullus, dives et Ancus," not "dives Tullus," observing that there is no just cause for calling Tullus rich, whereas the riches of Ancus were celebrated. Munro adopts Ritter's collocation.

Damna tamen celeres reparant cælestia lunæ;*
    Nos, ubi decidimus,
Quo pater Æneas, quo Tullus,** dives et Ancus,
    Pulvis et umbra sumus. †

Quis scit, an adjiciant hodiernæ crastina summæ
    Tempora di superi?
Cuncta manus avidas fugient heredis, amico
    Quæ dederis animo.

Cum semel occideris, et de te splendida § Minos
    Fecerit arbitria,
Non, Torquate, genus, non te facundia, non te
    Restituet pietas;

Infernis neque enim tenebris Diana pudicum
    Liberat Hippolytum;
Nec Lethæa valet Theseus abrumpere caro
    Vincula Pirithoo.

---

† *I.e.*, dust in the tomb, and a shade in Hades.

§ "'Splendida,' an epithet more proper of the court and tribunal than of the judgment (arbitria) given. . . . The choice of poetic figure by which to enlarge the simple notion, 'cum semel occideris,' was probably suggested by Torquatus's own profession as an advocate, alluded to in Ep. I. v. 8, 9."—YONGE. Ritter takes the epithet as referring to the splendour which surrounded the tribunal of Minos, enabling him more searchingly to inspect the souls whom he judged; and observes that the splendour is here opposed to "tenebris," line 25.

ODE VIII.

TO CENSORINUS.

On stated times, as in the Kalends of March and January, it was the custom of the wealthier Romans to make presents to their friends. To this custom Horace refers,

Goblets and bronzes rare, my Censorinus,
  I on my friends would heartily bestow;
I'd give them tripods, as Greece gave her heroes—
  Nor should the meanest of my gifts be thine,
Were I but rich in artful masterpieces
  Such as a Scopas or Parrhasius wrought, *
When one in stone, in liquid hues the other,
  Now fixed a mortal, now enshrined a god.
Not mine that wealth, † nor do such dainty treasures
  Fail to thine affluence nor allure thy mind;
That which charms *thee* is song: song I can proffer,
  And set a value on the gift I bring.
Marbles inscribed with a state's grateful praises,
  Wherein great chieftains live and breathe again:
The flights§ of Hannibal, his threats hurled backward,
  And impious Carthage perishing in flames,

---

* Scopas was a famous sculptor of Paros, according to Pausanias, flourishing about 450 years B. C. Parrhasius, a painter, native of Ephesus, about 400 B. C. He was a contemporary and rival of Zeuxis.

refers, sending his verses to Censorinus, as the most acceptable gift he could offer. C. Marcus Censorinus was a man of consular rank, bore a high reputation, and died greatly regretted.

Carm. VIII.

Donarem pateras grataque commodus,
Censorine, meis æra sodalibus;
Donarem tripodas, præmia fortium
Graiorum; neque tu pessima munerum
Ferres, divite me scilicet artium,
Quas aut Parrhasius protulit, aut Scopas, *
Hic saxo, liquidis ille coloribus
Sollers nunc hominem ponere, nunc deum.
Sed non hæc mihi vis; † non tibi talium
Res est, aut animus deliciarum egens.
Gaudes carminibus; carmina possumus
Donare, et pretium dicere muneri.
Non incisa notis marmora publicis,
Per quæ spiritus et vita redit bonis
Post mortem ducibus; non celeres fugæ, §
Rejectæque retrorsum Hannibalis minæ,

---

† "Sed non hæc mihi vis." The sense is approached by our English idiomatic slang expression, "I am not of that force."

§ "Celeres fugæ" means Hannibal's hasty recall from Italy (Liv. xxx. 20).—ORELLI.

Made not more famed than did Calabrian Muses
    Him who bore off from conquered Africa
As his own spoils—a Name.* Nor aught thy guerdon,
    If scrolls be mute upon thy deeds of good.
Though son of Mars and Ilia, what—had silence
    Been his worth's cold obstruction—Romulus?
The genius, favour, voice of powerful poets
    Consecrate Æacus, from waves of Styx
Ravished to golden isles.† The Muse permits not
    The mortal worthy of her praise to die;
Him the Muse hallows to the bliss of heaven.
    Thus in the longed-for banquet-hall of Jove

---

* "Scipio Africanus." This passage has given infinite trouble to the commentators. Ennius (denoted here by the "Calabrian Muses") celebrated the elder Scipio. But Carthage was burned, not by the elder Scipio, but by the younger Scipio Africanus, many years after the death of Ennius; and it cannot be supposed that Horace was so ignorant as to ascribe to the elder Scipio the act of the younger. It was even proposed by Bentley to omit the seventeenth verse, referring to Carthage, altogether; but the line is in all the MSS. extant. Others suggest that two lines are wanting after the seventeenth, which would have removed the alleged confusion; and this theory is supported by the assertion that odes in this measure are so constituted as to be reducible to stanzas of four lines each, while this ode wants at present two verses necessary to establish that rule. But, as Macleane observes, "the rule itself is arbitrary, and a precarious foundation for such an assumption as the loss of two verses, of which no traces are to be found in the oldest MSS. and commentators." Macleane thinks "that the confusion is easily seen through by those who avoid the commentators and judge for themselves. . . . When Horace says that the defeat of Hannibal by the elder Scipio, and the destruction of Carthage by the younger, do not hold up their name more nobly than the Muse of Calabria,—who does not supply, in his own mind, 'which was employed in doing honour to the elder'?" To me the meaning seems clear

BOOK IV.—ODE VIII.

Non incendia Carthaginis impiæ,
Ejus, qui domita nomen ab Africa *
Lucratus rediit, clarius indicant
Laudes, quam Calabræ Pierides: neque,
Si chartæ sileant, quod bene feceris,
Mercedem tuleris. Quid foret Iliæ
Mavortisque puer, si taciturnitas
Obstaret meritis invida Romuli?
Ereptum Stygiis fluctibus Æacum
Virtus et favor et lingua potentium
Vatum divitibus consecrat insulis. †
Dignum laude virum Musa vetat mori:

enough. Just as Horace, Lib. I., Carm. xii. v. 46, makes the name of Marcellus, who took Syracuse, stand for all his family, and include the young Marcellus, so he here makes the name of Africanus stand for the whole family, and include especially the younger Scipio. Or, as Ritter expresses it, the fame of the elder Scipio, recorded by Ennius, was revived in the destruction of Carthage by the younger.

† "Virtus et favor et lingua potentium
Vatum divitibus consecrat insulis."

"'Virtus et favor' are generally taken, like, 'lingua,' as belonging to 'potentium vatum,' so that 'virtus' is 'vis ingenii, facultas poetica.' I doubt the accuracy of that interpretation; I think it rather means that though Æacus was virtuous (and he was much celebrated for his justice), his virtue would not have raised him to the skies but for the applause won him by the poets. The causes, therefore, are, his virtue and the public esteem ('favor'), and the poet's praise that made his virtue known."—MACLEANE. This interpretation is very ingenious, but as it is opposed to that accepted by the general body of Horatian commentators, I do not admit it in translation, though, like all the suggestions of this eminent critic, it merits respectful attention. I may add that Ritter also separates "virtus" and "favor" from "lingua potentium vatum."

Sits resolute Hercules; the sons of Leda
    Thus—one twin-star—from Ocean's nether deep
Snatch tempest-shattered barks; and thus doth Liber,
    His brows adorned with the vine's lusty green,
Hear as a god our mortal supplications,
    And guide the votive prayer to happy ends.

Cælo Musa beat. Sic Jovis interest
Optatis epulis impiger Hercules
Clarum Tyndaridæ sidus ab infimis
Quassas eripiunt æquoribus rates;
Ornatus viridi tempora pampino
Liber vota bonos ducit ad exitus.

ODE IX.

TO LOLLIUS.

As the preceding poem was addressed to a man who retained unblemished a popular reputation to the last, and whose death was considered a public calamity, so this poem, which equally treats of the immortality it is the gift of poets to bestow, is addressed to one who, if we are to take for granted such historical records of him as are left, was the subject of merited obloquy in his later years, and died by poison which he administered to himself, to the great joy of his countrymen. And it was for the vices most opposite to the special virtues Horace here ascribes to Lollius —viz., for rapacity and corruption—that his character, rightly or wrongly, has been most defamed. His vindication has been, however, very ably attempted by Tate ('Vindiciæ Lollianæ'), and the evidence against him is generally considered to rest upon prejudiced and

Lest, perchance, thou believe that the words which to music,
I, whose birth was where Aufidus rushes far-sounding,
   Linked by arts not before me divulged,
     Are but sounds that are fated to die;

Remember, that though the first throne be great Homer's,
There are muses not tuneless, Pindaric and Cæan;-
   With Alcæus, yet threatening and fierce;
     With Stesichorus, stately and grave.

and questionable authority.—See Estré, Hor. Pros. At all events it is clear that the vices imputed to him by his personal enemy, Sulpicius Quirinus, and Velleius Paterculus, the adulator of Tiberius, were not suspected by Augustus, with whom, even after his defeat by the Sygambri, A.U.C. 737, he retained eminent favour and influence, and who subsequently appointed him tutor to his grandson, Caius Cæsar. If Lollius could deceive Augustus as to his real nature, it has been shrewdly observed that he might well deceive Horace. The exact date of the ode is unknown, but it has the appearance of being written after Lollius's defeat and recall; at all events, it was published not long after it, and is therefore an evidence of Horace's generous desire to soothe and sustain his friend in a time of reverse, and, no doubt, of unpopularity. The latter part of the poem is in Horace's noblest style of sentiment and expression. Ritter maintains that Epistles II. and XVIII., Lib. I., are addressed to the Lollius of the ode; but most critics consider them to be addressed to his eldest son.

CARM. IX.

Ne forte credas interitura, quæ
Longe sonantem natus ad Aufidum,
   Non ante volgatas per artes
     Verba loquor socianda chordis:

Non, si priores Mæonius tenet
Sedes Homerus, Pindaricæ latent,
   Ceæque, et Alcæi minaces,
     Stesichorique graves Camenæ;

Time destroys not what once sported loose in Anacreon;
To this day breathes the love, to this day glows the ardour,
   Which the girl of Æolia consigned
      To the strings of her passionate lyre.

Spartan Helen was not the sole woman inflamed by
An adulterer's sleek locks; or seduced by the glitter
   Of the vestments embroidered in gold,
      And the graces and pomp of a prince;

Teucer bent not the first skilful bow of the Cretan;
Troy was more than once harassed by valiant besiegers;
   Other chiefs, besides Sthenelus strong,
      Or Idomeneus mighty, achieved

Deeds as worthy as theirs of a Muse to record them;
Not the first was Deiphobus keen, or fierce Hector,
   Who has met, without flinching, the blow,
      In defence of his children and wife.

Many brave men have lived long before Agamemnon,
But o'er them darkly presses the slumber eternal;
   All unwept and unknown, wanting Him—
      Everlastingly sacred—the Bard!

Little differs worth hidden from worthlessness buried;
In the page I shall speak, and the page shall adorn thee;
   I will let not, O Lollius, thy toils
      Fade in livid oblivion away.

BOOK IV.—ODE IX.

Nec, si quid olim lusit Anacreon,
Delevit ætas; spirat adhuc amor,
   Vivuntque commissi calores
     Æoliæ fidibus puellæ.

Non sola comptos arsit adulteri
Crines, et aurum vestibus illitum
   Mirata, regalesque cultus
     Et comites Helene Lacæna;

Primusve Teucer tela Cydonio
Direxit arcu; non semel Ilios
   Vexata; non pugnavit ingens
     Idomeneus Sthenelusve solus

Dicenda Musis prœlia; non ferox
Hector, vel acer Deiphobus graves
   Excepit ictus pro pudicis
     Conjugibus puerisque primus.

Vixere fortes ante Agamemnona
Multi; sed omnes illacrimabiles
   Urgentur ignotique longa
     Nocte, carent quia vate sacro.

Paullum sepultæ distat inertiæ
Celata virtus. Non ego te meis
   Chartis inornatum silebo,
     Totve tuos patiar labores

In thy mind thou conjoinest life's practical knowledge,
And a temper unmoved by the changes of fortune,*
  Whatsoever her smile or her frown,
    Neither bowed nor elate,—but erect;

The avenger of greedy and fraudful Corruption,
The abstainer from Gold, which draws all to its magnet—
  Consul not of the one year alone,
    For thy mind must be always in power

Whensoever an arbiter, faithful to justice,
Over what is expedient exalts what is honest,
  Awes the briber with one lofty look,
    And through hosts clears, victorious, his way.†

It is not large possessions themselves that are blessings;
More rightly called "blest," he whose claim to the title
  Is the wisdom which puts to their use
    All the gifts that he owes to the gods,

---

* "Secundis
    Temporibus dubiisque rectus."

I agree with Orelli and Macleane in thinking these lines refer to the defeat of Lollius in Germany; and it seems that not only Horace here emphatically seeks to pay tribute to the steadfastness and integrity of his friend's character, but in the concluding stanza to vindicate his courage, and intimate that he was the last man who would have feared death.

† The meaning of these lines seems explained by reference to Lib. III. Od. II. lines 19, 20,—

    "Nec sumit aut ponit secures
      Arbitrio popularis auræ;"

i.e., Lollius is not the mere official consul of a single year—he never

Impune, Lolli, carpere lividas
Obliviones. Est animus tibi
   Rerumque prudens, et secundis
      Temporibus dubiisque rectus;*

Vindex avaræ fraudis, et abstinens
Ducentis ad se cuncta pecuniæ;
   Consulque non unius anni,
      Sed quoties bonus atque fidus

Judex honestum prætulit utili,
Rejecit alto dona nocentium
   Voltu, per obstantes catervas
      Explicuit sua victor arma.†

Non possidentem multa vocaveris
Recte beatum: rectius occupat
   Nomen beati, qui deorum
      Muneribus sapienter uti,

lays down the insignia of his majestic virtue. It seems to me that the image is still continued through the lines,—
    "Per obstantes catervas
    Explicuit sua victor arma."
The lictors dispersed opposing crowds to make way for the consul; and "arma" here may signify their axes. Yonge renders the passage yet more symbolically, in this eloquent paraphrase: "The soul has an independent dignity so long as, true in principle and judgment, it rejects corruption, and bursts in a moral victory through the host of vices." Ritter insists on construing the lines literally, and refers them to Lollius's military administration of his province.

He who hardens his soul to reverse and privation—
He who looks upon death as less dread than dishonour—
   Never fears, for the friends of his love
     Or the cause of his country, to die.

Duramque callet pauperiem pati,
Pejusque leto flagitium timet;
　Non ille pro caris amicis
　　Aut patria timidus perire.

ODE X. OMITTED.

ODE XI.

TO PHYLLIS.

As Horace had before (Lib. III. Od. xxviii.) invited Lyde to the feast-day of Neptune, so he here invites Phyllis to celebrate the birthday of Mæcenas in the Ides of April. The date of the ode cannot be determined, though it may be reasonably conjectured that when he speaks of Phyllis as his last love, he was of an age correspondent with the period at which the Fourth Book was published. Nevertheless this is no sure index; for, as Macleane shrewdly intimates, most men promise the women they woo that she shall be the last love. To those who insist upon giving literal individual personality to the fictitious names Horace introduces into his poems, this poem would seem written at a much earlier period, since Telephus, that universal ladykiller, is still described as "juvenis." But we have already seen that "juvenis" by no means necessarily signifies a youth. I do not believe, with Macleane,

I've a cask of rich Alban wine full in my cellar—
It has passed its ninth year; in my garden, fair Phyllis,
There is parsley for chaplets, and O, in profusion,
    Ivy too, ivy,

Thou art dazzling whenever that binds up thy tresses.
All my house laughs with plate; clasped around with
    chaste vervain,
Lo, mine altar stands thirsting the blood of a lambkin
    Soon to be sprinkled.

Macleane, that Telephus is altogether a poetic fiction; neither am I satisfied with the grounds upon which Ritter identifies the Telephus of Ode XIII. Book I., and XIX. Book III., with Heliodorus, the grammarian and Greek scholar mentioned Serm. I. 5, 2, and assumes that another person is designated under that name in this ode. Nothing is more likely than that among Horace's gayer companions there was some one very good-looking gallant, celebrated for his *bonnes fortunes* among the freedwomen of Rome, whom the poet always designates under the name of Telephus. It is observable that there is considerable consistency in the way in which Telephus is mentioned in Horace, with a good-humoured, half-envious admiration for personal gifts, and whom, on the single occasion (Carm. xix. Lib. III.) in which the handsome gentleman seems disposed to bore with an unseasonable display of learning, he puts back into his right place as reveller and gallant, with a certain superiority, such as, when it came to a display of learning, a Horace might be disposed to assume towards a Telephus.

Carm. XI.

Est mihi nonum superantis annum
Plenus Albani cadus; est in horto,
Phylli, nectendis apium coronis;
    Est hederæ vis

Multa, qua crines religata fulges;
Ridet argento domus; ara castis
Vincta verbenis avet immolato
    Spargier agno;

And all hands are at work; here and there run the
    servants,
Men and maids, helter-skelter; the flame mounts in
    flicker,
As it whirls the smoke cresting the point of its summit
    Round and around it.*

But that now thou mayst know to what mirth I invite
    thee,
'Tis in honour of Ides, not ungrateful to Phyllis,
'Tis the day that halves April, sweet month in which Venus
    Rose out of ocean;

Day, indeed, that by me should be solemnised duly—
Scarce mine own natal day I hold equally sacred,
Since it is by its light, year on year, my Mæcenas
    Sums up life's riches.

Come, that Telephus whom thou art seeking (poor
    Phyllis!
He's a youth above thee) is now chained to another.
She is wanton and rich, and she holds him in bondage,
    Pleased with his fetters.

Phaëthon, burnt in his chariot, deters from ambition,
Wingèd Pegasus spurning Bellerophon earth-born
May admonish thee also by this solemn lesson,
    "Seek but what suits thee;"

* "Sordidum flammæ trepidant relantes
            Vertice fumum."
"'Vertice' is the top of the flame, which flickers as it whirls the

Cuncta festinat manus, huc et illuc
Cursitant mixtæ pueris puellæ;
Sordidum flammæ trepidant rotantes
    Vertice fumum.*

Ut tamen noris, quibus advoceris
Gaudiis, Idus tibi sunt agendæ,
Qui dies mensem Veneris marinæ
    Findit Aprilem;

Jure sollemnis mihi, sanctiorque,
Pæne natali proprio, quod ex hac
Luce Mæcenas meus adfluentes
    Ordinat annos.

Telephum, quem tu petis, occupavit,
Non tuæ sortis juvenem, puella
Dives et lasciva, tenetque grata
    Compede vinctum.

Terret ambustus Phaëthon avaras
Spes; et exemplum grave præbet ales
Pegasus, terrenum equitem gravatus
    Bellerophontem;

---

dark smoke on its crest—a spiral flame, culminating in a column of smoke. It seems as if Horace were writing with a fire burning before him, and caught the idea as he wrote."—MACLEANE.

Deeming Hope, when it flies out of reach, is unlawful,
O set not thy heart where the lots are unequal.
Come, with me be contented, of all loves my latest;
    Love with thee endeth.

After thee never more woman's face shall inflame me;
O, be cheered, then, and come; let me teach thee such
        measures
As the voice which I love into sweetness shall render;
    Song lessens sorrow.

Semper ut te digna sequare, et ultra
Quam licet sperare nefas putando
Disparem vites.   Age jam, meorum
    Finis amorum,

Non enim posthac alia calebo
Femina,—condisce modos, amanda
Voce quos reddas; minuentur atræ
    Carmine curæ.

ODE XII.

INVITATION TO VIRGIL.

It is a vexed question among commentators whether the Virgil here addressed be Virgil the poet. Yonge says that the general authority of critics is against that identification. Macleane is disposed to favour it, and it is not without other and very eminent defenders.

The main objections to the assumption are—1st, the chronological one. Virgil was dead many years before the publication of the Fourth Book; but, in answer to this, it is said that, in making up the collection composed for Book IV., Horace might have included poems composed at a much earlier date. Dillenburger considers that this ode was written in youth, and published in the final book of the Odes, as if Horace wished to refresh and record the memory of his friend.

2d, It is asked, "How can Virgil the poet be called the client of noble youths?" To this it has been replied, that the youths referred to might be the stepsons of Augustus, or (more generally by Dillenburger), that the phrase means nothing more than the familiarity with persons of high station, such as Agrippa, Pollio, and others.

3d, That an injunction to lay aside the care or study of gain (studium lucri) is very inappropriate to the liberal and generous character assigned to the poet. But here again it is said, that it is absurd to take literally what is obviously written in jest. If a man, the most indifferent to gain, had, for instance, informed us that he thought he could sell an olive crop well, or that he had found a good investment for his money, we might very well say to him, "Put aside those mercenary thoughts of gain, and come and sup with us." There would be at once a jest and a compliment in the irony of the implied accusation. That the Virgil addressed must be a vender of perfumes, because he is asked to contribute a pot of nard; or a banker or negotiator, because he is exhorted to put aside the care of gain—and a scholiast in a Paris MS. inscribes the ode, "Ad Virgilium Negotiatorem,"—is a conjecture less plausible than that he was a physician of that name to the Neros, or a relation of C. Virgil the prætor, Cicero's friend.

Orelli and Yonge quote with approval Gesner's remark, "That there is nothing in the poem itself which pertains more to the poet Virgil than to any other friend of Horace's." On the other hand, it has been said that the mythological imagery and the description of Spring with which the poem opens, are addressed with appropriate felicity to the Poet of the Eclogues and Georgics.

The question does not seem to admit of positive solution one way or the other. The reader must judge for himself whether it is probable that Horace included in the Fourth Book a poem that, if addressed to Virgil the poet, he must have written many years before; and whether if he did thus, as Dillenburger contends, seek to revive the memory of his early friend, it would have been in a poem of a comparatively light character, and so wholly free from any reference to the loss he had sustained.

Now Thracian breezes, comrades of the spring,
Temper the ocean and impel the sails;
Frost crisps not now the fields, nor rage the floods,
    Swollen with winter snows.

Now builds her nest the melancholy bird
Yet moaning Itys; she, the eternal shame
Of Cecrops' house for vengeance too severe
    On barbarous lusts of kings.*

Swains of sleek flocks on the young grass reclined,
Chant pastoral songs attuned to piping reeds,
Charming the god who loves the darksome slopes
    And folds of Arcady;

These, O my Virgil, are the days of thirst;
But if, O client of illustrious youths,
Calenian juices tempt, bring thou the nard,
    And with it earn my wine;

One tiny box of spikenard will draw forth
The cask now ripening in Sulpician† vaults,—
Cask large enough to hold a world of hope,
    And drown a world of care.

---

* "Quod male barbaras,
    Regum est ulta libidines."

Most authorities, Orelli amongst them, take "male" with "ulta" —viz., that the bird, whether Philomela or Procne, avenged too cruelly (nimis atrociter) the guilt of Tereus. I have translated accordingly, but am by no means sure that "male" should not be taken, as Macleane suggests, with "barbaras"—viz., the too barbarous, or evilly barbarous, lusts of kings. The bird is the eternal reproach to the house of Cecrops, not on account of the severity of her vengeance, but on account of the atrocity of the crimes she avenged. Most commentators of authority agree that the bird here

Carm. XII.

Jam Veris comites, quæ mare temperant,
Impellunt animæ lintea Thraciæ;
Jam nec prata rigent nec fluvii strepunt
    Hiberna nive turgidi.

Nidum ponit, Ityn flebiliter gemens,
Infelix avis et Cecropiæ domus
Æternum opprobrium, quod male barbaras
    Regum est ulta libidines.*

Dicunt in tenero gramine pinguium
Custodes ovium carmina fistula,
Delectantque deum, cui pecus et nigri
    Colles Arcadiæ placent.

Adduxere sitim tempora, Virgili;
Sed pressum Calibus ducere Liberum
Si gestis, juvenum nobilium cliens,
    Nardo vina merebere.

Nardi parvus onyx eliciet cadum,
Qui nunc Sulpiciis accubat horreis,†
Spes donare novas largus, amaraque
    Curarum eluere efficax.

---

meant is the swallow, not nightingale. Ritter understands by "flebiliter" the swallow's inarticulate twitter.

† "Sulpiciis horreis." The Sulpician wine-vaults were famous, and the scholiast Porphyrion says they were still the great magazines for wine and oil in his day, under the name of the Galban cellars. Ritter considers that Orelli is mistaken in supposing that Horace intimates that he will *buy* the wine there; and maintains that he refers to his own cask, which had been warehoused in the Sulpician magazine.

Quick! if such merriments delight thee, come
With thine own contributions to the feast;
Not like rich host in prodigal halls—my cups
    Thou shalt not tinge scot-free.

But put aside delays and care of gain,
Warned, while yet time, by the dark death-fires; mix
With thought brief thoughtlessness; to be unwise
    In time and place is sweet.

Ad quæ si properas gaudia, cum tua
Velox merce veni: non ego te meis
Immunem meditor tingere poculis,
    Plena dives ut in domo.

Verum pone moras et studium lucri,
Nigrorumque memor, dum licet, ignium,
Misce stultitiam consiliis brevem:
    Dulce est desipere in loco.

ODE XIII.

TO LYCE, A FADED BEAUTY.

No subject of inquiry can be less interesting to a critic of good sense than that on which so many learned disputants have wasted their time—viz., who among the ladies celebrated by Horace were real persons or imaginary; and who are to be admitted into or rejected from the genuine catalogue of his loves? We have absolutely no data to go upon. There is no reason, except that he chooses to apply the same name to both, to suppose that the Lyce over whose ruined charms he now exults was the Lyce of whose cruelty he complains, Lib. III. Od. x.; nay, I believe that most recent scholars are pretty well agreed that the ode last mentioned was an artistic exercise, imitated from the Greek serenades. But, so far as mere conjecture from internal evidence may be allowed, the

> They have heard my prayers, Lyce, the gods;
> The gods have heard, Lyce; thou'rt old,
>   Yet still, setting up for a beauty,
>   Thou wouldst tipple and frisk with the young;
>
> Courting, maudlin, with tremulous chant,
> Laggard Cupid: he's absent on guard
>   O'er the bloom on the cheeks of young Chia,
>   Whose lute is more sweet than thy song.*

* There is an opposition between Lyce's tremulous quaver, "cantu tremulo," and Chia's musical skill, "doctæ psallere,"

the present ode seems to have in it a tone of earnestness which warrants a belief that the Lyce addressed was a real person. In the three concluding stanzas, the bitterness of sarcasm is tinged with a certain melancholy pathos which appears to indicate the memory of a former passion; and the direct reference to Cinara—to whom all interpreters agree in considering Horace was attached (whether or not he celebrates her under names of the same metrical quantity, Lalage, Glycera, &c.)—gives a peculiar air of individual truthfulness to the poem. Be this as it may, the ode is remarkable for its eternal applicability to a type in female character, and is replete with beauties of expression. The image in the last stanza is extremely striking. The simile is so simple that one might fancy it would have occurred to any poet, yet it is so expressed as to be quite original.

CARM. XIII.

Audivere, Lyce, di mea vota, di
Audivere, Lyce; fis anus, et tamen
   Vis formosa videri,
     Ludisque et bibis impudens,

Et cantu tremulo pota Cupidinem
Lentum sollicitas. Ille virentis et
   Doctæ psallere Chiæ
     Pulchris excubat in genis.*

---

* which can only, perhaps, be made clear by some slight paraphrase, as is attempted in the last line of the stanza, in translation.

For he roosts not on oaks without sap;
Hollow teeth and dry wrinkles he flies,
    He is chilled by the snow of grey tresses,
        And thus has retreated from thee.

Sparkling gems, and the purples of Cos,*
Cannot back to thee bring the dead years
    Rapid Time has interred in our annals,
        For all men to number their graves.†

Whither fled is the beauty? alas!
Where the bloom? where the movement of grace?
    Of that—O of that—what is left thee,
        Breathing loves, which stole me from myself,

Blest successor to Cinara thou,
Gracious form,§ for arts pleasing renowned?
    But to Cinara few years were conceded,
        By the Fates who have Lyce preserved

To be rival in age to the crow,
That the young, glowing yet, may behold,
    As a subject of mirth, in those ashes
        The fallen remains of a torch.

---

* Horace speaks of the robes from Cos in Sat. I. II. line 100, as so transparent that they left nothing to conceal.

† "Tempora, quæ semel
    Notis condita fastis
        Inclusit volucris dies."

"Horace means to say that the days she has seen are all buried, as it were, in the grave of the public annals (as Acron says), and there any one may find them, but she cannot get them back. It is a graphic way of identifying the years, and marking their decease,

Importunus enim transvolat aridas
Quercus, et refugit te, quia luridi
　　Dentes, te quia rugæ
　　　Turpant et capitis nives.

Nec Coæ referunt jam tibi purpuræ,*
Nec clari lapides tempora, quæ semel
　　Notis condita fastis
　　　Inclusit volucris dies.†

Quo fugit Venus? heu, quove color? decens
Quo motus? quid habes illius, illius,
　　Quæ spirabat Amores,
　　　Quæ me surpuerat mihi,

Felix post Cinaram, notaque et artium
Gratarum facies?§ Sed Cinaræ breves
　　Annos fata dederunt,
　　　Servatura diu parem

Cornicis vetulæ temporibus Lycen;
Possent ut juvenes visere fervidi,
　　Multo non sine risu,
　　　Dilapsam in cineres facem.

to point to the record in which each is distinguished by its consuls and its leading events. 'Notis' merely expresses the publicity and notoriety of the record by which the lapse of time is marked."—MACLEANE.

　　　§ "Notaque et artium
　　　　Gratarum facies?"

"'Facies' does not mean the face alone, but the whole form and presence. 'Facies autem totam corporis speciem significat.'"—DILLENBURGER. See, too, Orelli's note.

ODE XIV.

TO AUGUSTUS, AFTER THE VICTORIES OF TIBERIUS.

The introduction to Ode IV. in this book has, sufficiently for the purpose, sketched the outline of the events

By what care can the Senate of Rome, and Rome's people,
With a largess of honours sufficiently ample,
  By what titles, what archives to time,
    Eternise thy virtues, Augustus,

Prince supremest, wherever the sun lights a region
That man can inhabit? What in war thou availest,
  The Vindelici lately have learned,
    Free till then from the law of the Roman.

By no even exchange in the barter of bloodshed,*
Drusus, leading thy hosts, overthrew the fleet Breuni—
  The Genauni—implacable race—
    And the citadels piled upon Alps

Horror-breathing; then Nero the elder completed
Glories due to thine auspice in one crowning battle;
  Closed the raid of the savage, and crushed
    The grim might of the giant-like Ræti.

---

* "Plus vice simplici." This does not mean "more than once," but, as the scholiasts interpret, "with double loss to the

events which led to the composition of this ode. As the former was devoted to the praises of Drusus, so the latter commemorates the subsequent and completing conquests of Tiberius, and refers all to the honour of Augustus in the establishment of his empire, and the consummation of his fortunes and his glory.

CARM. XIV.

Quæ cura Patrum, quæve Quiritium,
Plenis honorum muneribus tuas,
    Auguste, virtutes in ævum
        Per titulos memoresque fastos

Æternet, O, qua sol habitabiles
Illustrat oras, maxime principum?
    Quem legis expertes Latinæ,
        Vindelici didicere nuper,

Quid Marte posses. Milite nam tuo
Drusus Genaunos, implacidum genus,
    Breunosque veloces, et arces
        Alpibus impositas tremendis,

Dejecit acer plus vice simplici;[a]
Major Neronum mox grave prœlium
    Commisit, immanesque Rætos
        Auspiciis pepulit secundis:

---

enemy;" or literally, as Macleane renders it, "with more than an even exchange"—*i.e.*, of blood.

All conspicuous he rode where the fight raged the
 fiercest,
Wasting down, to what wrecks! that array of stern
 bosoms,
   Self-surrendered as offerings to death,
     In the stubborn devotion to freedom.

Through the foe went his way, as the blast o'er the
 billows
When the Pleiads are cleaving the rain-clouds asunder,
   And the snort of his war-horse was heard
     In the midst of the lightnings of battle.*

As when Aufidus, laving the kingdoms of Daunus,
Bursts in wrath, and in form of the wild bull,† his
 borders,
   And prepares the dread deluge he drives
     O'er the fields that are rife with the harvest,—

So in storm, through that barbarous array swept the
 Nero,
Mowing, foremost to hindmost, ranks serried in iron,
   Till a victor he stood, without loss,
     On a ground that was strewn with the foemen;

But he owed to thyself the resources, the counsels,
And the gods. From the day that her gates and void
 palace,
   Suppliant Egypt threw open to thee,
     Had thy reign reached its third happy lustre,

---

* "Medios per ignes"—*i.e.*, "per medium ardorem belli"
(COM. CRUQ.)

Spectandus in certamine Martio,
Devota morti pectora liberæ
   Quantis fatigaret ruinis;
      Indomitas prope qualis undas

Exercet Auster, Pleïadum choro
Scindente nubes, impiger hostium
   Vexare turmas, et frementem
      Mittere equum medios per ignes. *

Sic tauriformis volvitur Aufidus, †
Qui regna Dauni præfluit Apuli,
   Cum sævit, horrendamque cultis
      Diluviem meditatur agris,

Ut barbarorum Claudius agmina
Ferrata vasto diruit impetu,
   Primosque et extremos metendo
      Stravit humum, sine clade victor,

Te copias, te consilium et tuos
Præbente divos. Nam tibi, quo die
   Portus Alexandrea supplex
      Et vacuam patefecit aulam,

---

† "Tauriformis Aufidus;" literally, "tauriform" or "bull-formed Aufidus." The image is applied to many rivers by the Greek and Latin poets. Macleane suggests that the branches of so many large streams at the mouths of rivers might have suggested the idea of the horns; but it seems to me that the comparison to the bull in general applies to the blind and senseless violence of the animal, who runs on indiscriminately, trampling and destroying everything in his way—just as the inundation of a torrent does.

When, in crowning thy wish and completing thy glory,
Fortune ended the wars which her favour had prospered,*
   And established in triumph the peace
     Of a world underneath thy dominion.

Thee the dauntless Cantabrian, before never conquered;
Thee the Mede and the Indian, and Scyth, the wild Nomad,
   Mark in wonder and awe, guardian shield
     Of Italia, and Rome the earth's mistress.

Thee the Nile, unrevealing the source of its waters;
Thee the Danube; and thee the swift rush of the Tigris;
   Thee the monster-fraught ocean, which roars
     Round the birthplace remote of the Briton;

Thee fierce Gallia, the land for which death has no terror,
Thee Iberia, the stubborn, hear hushed and submissive;
   The Sygambri, exulting in gore,
     With meek arms piled in trophy, adore thee.

---

* Horace, here addressing Augustus, ascribes it to him as his crowning victory that he has at last got the wish of his heart, which was peace—the peace of the world, subjected to the Roman Empire.

Fortuna lustro prospera tertio
Belli secundos reddidit exitus, *
   Laudemque et optatum peractis
     Imperiis decus arrogavit.

Te Cantaber non ante domabilis,
Medusque, et Indus, te profugus Scythes
   Miratur, O tutela præsens
     Italiæ dominæque Romæ:

Te, fontium qui celat origines
Nilusque et Ister, te rapidus Tigris,
   Te beluosus qui remotis
     Obstrepit Oceanus Britannis;

Te non paventis funera Galliæ
Duræque tellus audit Hiberiæ;
   Te cæde gaudentes Sygambri
     Compositis venerantur armis.

The victory of Tiberius was on the fifteenth anniversary of the day on which Augustus entered Alexandria, and, thus terminating the civil war, became supreme.

ODE XV.

TO AUGUSTUS ON THE RESTORATION OF PEACE.

This ode is the appropriate epilogue to the Fourth Book, of which the poems that celebrate the Roman victories under Drusus and Tiberius constitute the noblest portion. If it be true that the book was published on account of these odes, and at the desire of Augustus, Horace would naturally conclude by a special reference to the beneficial issues of the wars undertaken by Augustus, and from the final completion of which in Gaul, Germany, and Spain, he had just returned to Rome. Horace here begins by saying, that when he wished to sing of those wars, Phœbus checked him. But Phœbus does not forbid him to sing

Of wars and vanquished cities when I longed
To sing, Apollo checked me with his lyre,
  Lest I launched sails so slight
    Into so vast a deep. Cæsar, thy reign

Has given back golden harvests to our fields;
Our standards, torn from Parthia's haughty walls,
  Restored to Roman Jove;
    Closed gates of Janus, vacant of a war;

To righteous order rampant licence curbed,
Thrust from the state the vices* which defiled,
  And, in their stead, recalled
    The ancient virtues to their fatherland, †—

---

* "Emovitque culpas." This refers to the moral reforms undertaken by Augustus, such as the Julian law, "de adulteriis et de pudicitia."

sing the triumphs of peace; and, with a lively lyrical abruptness, he therefore at once bursts forth:—

"Tua, Cæsar, ætas
Fruges et agris retulit uberes," &c.

That the poem was composed immediately after the return of Cæsar, and in connection with Odes IV. and XIV., is, I think, made clear by its own internal evidence. War is finished, and Augustus is celebrated as the triumphant establisher of law and order, and the author of the national prosperity, and the improvements, social and moral, which result from the security to life and property bestowed by a government at once firm and beneficent. He is here the descendant, not of Mars and Ilia, but of Anchises and Venus the gentle.

CARM. XV.

Phœbus volentem prœlia me loqui
Victas et urbes, increpuit lyra;
   Ne parva Tyrrhenum per æquor
     Vela darem. Tua, Cæsar, ætas

Fruges et agris retulit uberes,
Et signa nostro restituit Jovi,
   Derepta Parthorum superbis
     Postibus, et vacuum duellis

Janum Quirini clausit, et ordinem
Rectum evaganti frena Licentiæ
   Injecit, emovitque culpas, *
     Et veteres revocavit artes, †

† "'Veteres artes.' 'Artes' here means 'virtues,' as in Book III. Od. III. 'Hac arte' (ἀρετῇ), as prudence, fortitude, justice, temperance."—ACRON.

Virtues from which have grown the Roman name,
Italia's might, fame, and majestic sway,
   To the Sun's Orient rise,
     From his calm bed in our Hesperian seas.

Cæsar our guardian, neither civil rage*
Nor felon violence scares us from repose,
   Nor ire which sharpens swords,
     And makes the wars of nations and their woes.

Neither the drinkers of deep Danube break
The Julian Laws, nor Scyths, nor Seres fierce,
   Nor Persia's faithless sons,
     Nor wild men cradled on the banks of Don.

So, with each sacred, with each common day
(Prayer, as is due, first rendered to the gods),
   'Mid blithesome Liber's boons,
     Gathering our women and our children round,

Let us, as did our fathers in old time,
Honour with hymns and Lydian fife brave chiefs:
   Sing Troy; Anchises sing;
     Sing of the race from gentle Venus sprung.

---

* "Non furor
Civilis aut vis exiget otium,
Non ira, quæ procudit enses,
Et miseras inimicat urbes."

Three causes of fear are removed: "Furor civilis," "civil war;" "vis," "personal violence;" "ira," "foreign wars."

Per quas Latinum nomen et Italæ
Crevere vires, famaque et imperi
    Porrecta majestas ad ortus
        Solis ab Hesperio cubili.

Custode rerum Cæsare, non furor
Civilis aut vis exiget otium,
    Non ira, quæ procudit enses,
        Et miseras inimicat urbes.*

Non, qui profundum Danubium bibunt,
Edicta rumpent Julia, non Getæ,
    Non Seres, infidive Persæ,
        Non Tanain prope flumen orti.

Nosque et profestis lucibus et sacris,
Inter jocosi munera Liberi,
    Cum prole matronisque nostris,
        Rite deos prius apprecati,

Virtute functos, more patrum, duces,
Lydis remixto carmine tibiis,
    Trojamque et Anchisen et almæ
        Progeniem Veneris canemus.

THE EPODES.

INTRODUCTION.

ORELLI, Dillenburger, and Macleane concur in accepting Franke's date for the publication of the book of Epodes—viz., A.U.C. 724, when Horace was thirty-five years old. The poems contained in the book appear to have been written between 713 and the date at which they were published; and, no doubt, many of them were known to Horace's friends before publication. It is to these Epodes that Horace refers in the boast, Epist. I. 19-23, that "He first introduced the Parian iambics, following the numbers and the spirit of Archilochus" (of Paros). Their title of Epode was not given to them (any more than that of Ode was given to the poems classed under that name) by Horace himself. Such designations are the inventions of some long-subsequent grammarian.

These poems are not lyrical in point of form, though they are occasionally so in point of spirit—especially, I think, the 13th Epode. They serve as an intermediate link between Horace's Odes and his earlier Satires.

The first ten Epodes are all in the same metre—alternate trimeter and dimeter iambics; they admit spondees only in the uneven places, and there is but one instance (II. 35) in which an anapæst is admitted.

INTRODUCTION. 219

In the translation, the metre selected for the more important of these Epodes has been employed in the version of a few of the graver odes—viz., the ordinary form of blank verse converted into a couplet by alternate terminations in a dissyllable and monosyllable.

In the lighter of these first ten Epodes—viz., Ep. VI. X.—I have thought that the variation of a more easy and rapid measure was necessary to represent the lively spirit of the Latin.

EPODE I.

TO MÆCENAS.

This epode is generally supposed to have been composed when Augustus had summoned the leading public men, whether senators or equites, to meet him at Brundusium prior to the expedition against Antony and Cleopatra which resulted in the battle of Actium, A.U.C. 723. The poem warrants the assumption that Mæcenas had been then appointed to, or offered, a naval command; but it seems (Dio. 51, 3, and Seneca, Ep. 114, 6) that Augustus decided on retaining him at home to watch over the affairs of Italy, and maintain order

So thou wilt go with thy Liburnian galleys,
    Amongst, O friend, those giant floating towers;
Prepared to share all perils braved by Cæsar,
    And ward them off, Mæcenas, by thine own.
But what of us, to whom, while thou survivest,
    Life is a joy;—thee lost, a weary load?
Shall we, as bidden, take our ease contented?
    Ease has no sweetness if not shared with thee;
Or shall we bear our part in thy great labour
    As fitting men of no unmanly mould?
Yes, we would bear; and thee o'er Alpine summits,
    Or through the wastes of guestless Caucasus,
Or where the last pale rim of the horizon
    Fades on the farthest waters of the west,
Follow with soul undaunted. Dost thou ask me
    How, weak in body, and unskilled in war,

order at Rome. Mr Dyer, in the 'Classical Museum,' vol. II. p. 199, and subsequently in Smith's 'Biographical Dictionary' (art. "Mæcenas"), contends that the poem refers to the Sicilian expedition against Sextus Pompeius, A.U.C. 718. Macleane objects to this supposition—"that the language of affection is too strong for the short acquaintance which Horace had then enjoyed with Mæcenas, and that there is evidence in the poem itself of the Sabine farm having come into Horace's possession when he wrote it; but that this did not occur till after the publication of the First Book of Satires is certain, and it is generally referred to A.U.C. 720."

CARM. I.

Ibis Liburnis inter alta navium,
    Amice, propugnacula,
Paratus omne Cæsaris periculum
    Subire, Mæcenas, tuo.
Quid nos, quibus te vita si superstite
    Jucunda, si contra, gravis?
Utrumne jussi persequemur otium,
    Non dulce, ni tecum simul,
An hunc laborem mente laturi, decet
    Qua ferre non molles viros?
Feremus; et te vel per Alpium juga
    Inhospitalem et Caucasum,
Vel Occidentis usque ad ultimum sinum
    Forti sequemur pectore.
Roges, tuum labore quid juvem meo,
    Imbellis ac firmus parum?

My toil could lighten thine? I should be present
　With terrors less than those the absent know;
Even as the bird more dreads for her young nestlings,
　If for a moment left, the gliding snake;
Not that her presence could avail for succour,
　Albeit she felt them underneath her wing.
Gladly in this or any war a soldier
　Would I enlist, for hope of thy dear grace;
Not that, attached by ampler teams of oxen,
　My ploughs may struggle through the stubborn glebe—
Not that my flocks should, ere the dog-star parcheth,
　Change hot Calabria for Lucanian slopes*—
Not that for me some villa's pomp of marble
　Should shine down white upon luxuriant vales,
Touching the walls with which the son of Circe†
　Girded enchanted land in Tusculum.
Enough, and more than I can need, for riches,
　Thanks to thy bounty, is already mine;
I am no Chremes, hoarding gold to bury§—
　No loose-robed spendthrift lusting gold to waste.

---

* The wealthy proprietors sent their flocks in summer from the hot Calabrian plains to the wooded hills of Lucania.

† Telegonus, son of Circe by Ulysses, said to have founded ancient Tusculum on the summit of the hill, the slope of which is occupied by the modern Frascati, and to have there introduced the magic arts of his mother. The lines in the original are slightly

Comes minore sum futurus in metu,
  Qui major absentes habet;
Ut assidens implumibus pullis avis
  Serpentium allapsus timet
Magis relictis; non, ut adsit, auxili
  Latura plus præsentibus.
Libenter hoc et omne militabitur
  Bellum in tuæ spem gratiæ;
Non ut juvencis illigata pluribus
  Aratra nitantur mea;
Pecusve Calabris ante sidus fervidum
  Lucana mutet pascuis;*
Neque ut superni villa candens Tusculi
  Circæa tangat mœnia.†
Satis superque me benignitas tua
  Ditavit: haud paravero,
Quod aut avarus ut Chremes terra premam,§
  Discinctus aut perdam nepos.

paraphrased in the translation, in order not to lose to the English reader the poetic idea associating Tusculum with legendary enchantment, which the words "Circæa mœnia" would have conveyed to the Latin.

  § "'Chremes.' The allusion is, perhaps, to a character in some play of Menander."—MACLEANE.

EPODE II.

ALFIUS.—THE CHARMS OF RURAL LIFE.

This poem, in which a glowing description of country life and its innocent attractions is placed in the mouth of the rich usurer Alfius, is one of the happiest examples of Horace's power of polished and latent irony. Macleane thinks that the poem was originally written in praise of rural life, and that the last lines were added to give the rest a moral. "At any rate," he says, "the greater part of the speech must be admitted to be rather out of keeping with the supposed speaker." This alleged want of keeping does not strike me, nor do I believe that the last lines were "an afterthought." The idea is in complete harmony with the substance of Satire I. Book I., in which Horace says that the miser is never contented with his own

"Blessed is he—remote, as were the mortals
  Of the first age, from business and its cares—
Who ploughs paternal fields with his own oxen
  Free from the bonds of credit or of debt.*

---

* "Solutus omni fenore"—"who neither lends nor borrows upon usury:" so Torrentius and Orelli. Macleane says the words would equally suit any other person besides a city usurer, and would mean that in the country he would not be subject to the calls of creditors, and need not get into debt. This interpretation is perhaps too loosely hazarded. An illustrious Horatian critic, to whom the translator is largely indebted, observes that "solutus" evidently

own lot, but rather extols those who follow opposite pursuits:—

"Nemo ut avarus
Se probet, ac potius laudet diversa sequentes;"

but that nevertheless the nature of the man returns to him; and if you offered to let him exchange with the person he envies, and so be happy, he would not accept the offer. The same idea is expressed more briefly, Book I. Ode I. lines 15, 35—"The merchant, terrified by the storms, lauds the ease of the country, but very soon refits his battered vessels." That a rich money-lender might at some moment feel and express very glowingly an enthusiasm for country life is natural enough; we have instances of that every day. No one praises or covets a country life more than a rich Jew or contractor. We do not know the occasion which may have suggested the poem; but nothing is more likely than that there was a report that the famous usurer was about to buy a country place and retire from business; and on the strength of that rumour Horace wrote the poem.

Carm. II.

'Beatus ille, qui procul negotiis,
　Ut prisca gens mortalium,
Paterna rura bobus exercet suis,
　Solutus omni fenore,*

---

refers to usurious bonds, and is so employed in the Satires; and suggests, as a more literal translation, "Unshackled by the bonds of usury."

No soldier he, roused by the savage trumpet,
  Not his to shudder at the angry sea;*
His life escapes from the contentious forum,
  And shuns the insolent thresholds of the great.
And so he marries to the amorous tendrils
  Of the young vine the poplar's lofty stem;
Or marks from far the lowing herds that wander
  Leisurely down the calm secluded vale;
Or, pruning with keen knife the useless branches,
  Grafts happier offspring on the parent tree;
Or in pure jars he stores the clear-prest honey;
  Or shears the fleeces of his tender sheep;†
Or, when brown Autumn from the fields uplifteth
  Brows with ripe coronal of fruits adorned,
What joy to pluck the pear himself hath grafted,
  And his own grape, that with the purple vies,
Wherewith he pays thee, rural god Priapus,
  And, landmark-guardian, Sire Silvanus, thee:§
Free to recline, now under aged ilex,
  Now in frank sunshine on the matted grass,
While through the steep banks slip the gliding waters,
  And birds are plaintive in the forest glens,
And limpid fountains, with a drowsy tinkle,
  Invite the light wings of the noonday sleep.

"But when the season of the storm, rude winter,
  Gathers together all its rains and snows,

---

* "Nec horret iratum mare." This does not apply to the sailor, but to the trader or merchant—"nec mercaturam exercet."
—ORELLI.

† "Aut tondet infirmas oves." Baxter strangely interprets "infirmas" as "sickly" (ægrotas); Orelli as "feeble" (imbecillas).

EPODE II.

Neque excitatur classico miles truci,
  Neque horret iratum mare,*
Forumque vitat et superba civium
  Potentiorum limina.
Ergo aut adulta vitium propagine
  Altas maritat populos,
Aut in reducta valle mugientium
  Prospectat errantes greges;
Inutilesque falce ramos amputans
  Feliciores inserit;
Aut pressa puris mella condit amphoris;
  Aut tondet infirmas oves; †
Vel, cum decorum mitibus pomis caput
  Auctumnus agris extulit,
Ut gaudet insitiva decerpens pira,
  Certantem et uvam purpuræ,
Qua muneretur te, Priape, et te, pater
  Silvane, tutor finium! §
Libet jacere, modo sub antiqua ilice,
  Modo in tenaci gramine.
Labuntur altis interim ripis aquæ,
  Queruntur in silvis aves,
Fontesque lymphis obstrepunt manantibus,
  Somnos quod invitet leves.
At cum Tonantis annus hibernus Jovis
  Imbres nivesque comparat,

Voss translates it "zarter," and so far agrees with Macleane, who considers it a purely ornamental expression.

§ "Pater Silvane, tutor finium." Silvanus, whose more usual attribute is the care of corn-fields and cattle, is here made to undertake the protection of boundaries, which properly belonged to Terminus.

Or here and there, into the toils before them,
  With many a hound he drives the savage boars;
Or with fine net, on forkèd stake suspended,
  Spreads for voracious thrushes fraudful snare,
And—joyful prizes—captures in his springes
  The shy hare and that foreigner the crane.
Who would not find in these pursuits oblivion
  Of all the baleful cares which wait on love?
Yet, if indeed he boasts an honest helpmate,
  Who, like the Sabine wife or sunburnt spouse
Of brisk Apulian, in the cares of household
  And of sweet children bears her joyous part;
Who on the sacred hearth the oldest fagots
  Piles 'gainst the coming of her wearied lord;
And in the wattled close the milch-kine penning,
  Drains the distended udders of their load;
From the sweet cask draws forth the year's new vintage,
  And spreads the luxuries of an unbought feast:
Such fare would charm me more than rarest dainties—
  Than delicate oyster of the Lucrine lake,
Or (if from eastern floods loud-booming winter
  Drive to our seas) the turbot or the scar.
Not softer sinks adown the grateful palate
  The Nubian pullet or the Ionian snipe,*
Than olives chosen where they hang the thickest;
  Or sorrel, lusty lover of green fields;
Or mallows, wholesome for the laden body,
  Or lambkin slain on Terminus' high feast,

---

* "Afra avis"—"attagen Ionicus." What bird is meant by the "Afra avis" is a matter of uncertainty. Yonge says it is the guinea-fowl—Macleane inclines to the same opinion; but we know little more of it than that it was speckled. The "attagen" is vari-

Aut trudit acres hinc et hinc multa cane
    Apros in obstantes plagas;
Aut amite levi rara tendit retia,
    Turdis edacibus dolos;
Pavidumque leporem et advenam laqueo gruem
    Jucunda captat præmia.
Quis non malarum, quas amor curas habet,
    Hæc inter obliviscitur?
Quod si pudica mulier in partem juvet
    Domum atque dulces liberos,
Sabina qualis, aut perusta solibus
    Pernicis uxor Apuli,
Sacrum vetustis exstruat lignis focum
    Lassi sub adventum viri;
Claudensque textis cratibus lætum pecus
    Distenta siccet ubera;
Et horna dulci vina promens dolio
    Dapes inemptas apparet:
Non me Lucrina juverint conchylia,
    Magisve rhombus, aut scari,
Si quos Eois intonata fluctibus
    Hiems ad hoc vertat mare;
Non Afra avis descendat in ventrem meum,
    Non attagen Ionicus*
Jucundior, quam lecta de pinguissimis
    Oliva ramis arborum,
Aut herba lapathi prata amantis, et gravi
    Malvæ salubres corpori,

ously interpreted woodcock, snipe, and, more commonly, moor-
fowl. The Ionian snipe is to this day so incomparably the best of
the snipe race, that I venture to think it is the veritable "attagen
Ionicus."

Or kidling rescued from the wolf's fierce hunger.
How sweet, amid such feasts, to view the sheep
Flock blithe from field to fold, see the tired oxen
  With languid neck draw back the inverted share,
And home-born* labourers round the shining Lares
  Gathered—the faithful swarm of the rich hive!"
Thus said the usurer Alfius, and all moneys
  Lent till the mid-month at that date calls in,
And, hot for rural pleasures, that day fortnight
  Our would-be farmer—lends them out again.†

---

* "Positosque vernas, ditis examen domus." This is a picture of the primitive rustic life, in which the labourers, familiarly with the master, gathered at supper round the Lares.—COLUM. XI. 1, 19. "The home-born slaves cluster round the master, as the bees round the queen-bee."—RITTER.

Vel agna festis caesa Terminalibus,
  Vel haedus ereptus lupo.
Has inter epulas, ut juvat pastas oves
  Videre properantes domum,
Videre fessos vomerem inversum boves
  Collo trahentes languido,
Positosque vernas, ditis examen domus,*
  Circum renidentes Lares!'
Haec ubi locutus fenerator Alfius,
  Jam jam futurus rusticus,
Omnem redegit Idibus pecuniam,—
  Quaerit Kalendis ponere.†

---

† "Omnem redegit Idibus pecuniam,—
  Quaerit Kalendis ponere."
The ides, nones, and kalends were the settling days of Rome.

EPODE III.

TO MÆCENAS IN EXECRATION OF GARLIC.

Horace appears to have been tempted to eat, when dining with Mæcenas, some dish over-seasoned with garlic, unaware of the prevalence of that ingredient, or unprescient of its effects. Some commentators, whom Dillenburger follows, suppose this to have been a kind of compound salad called "moretum," in which cheese, oil, milk, and wine contributed their motley aid to the garlic. This, however, was a primitive rustic comestible not likely to have been found at the table of Mæcenas. Whatever the dish might have been, Horace seems to have considered the recommendation of it a bad joke, and he takes revenge upon the

If e'er a parricide with hand accursèd
   Hath cut a father's venerable throat,
Hemlock's too mild a poison—give him garlic;
   O the strong stomachs of your country clowns!
What deadly drug is raging in my vitals?
   Was viper's venom in those fraudful herbs?
Or was Canidia, armed with all her poisons,
   The awful cook of that infernal feast?
Surely Medea, wonderstruck with Jason,
   As of all Argonauts the comeliest chief,*

---

* "Ut Argonautas præter omnes candidum
   Medea mirata est ducem."
"Postenquam Medea Jasonis ceteris omnibus Argonautis pulchrioris

the chief criminal, garlic, in the following humorous anathema.

The commentators in general assume that Horace could not have taken the liberty to refer to Terentia in the concluding lines, "Manum puella," &c., and that the poem was therefore written before Mæcenas's marriage, probably A.U.C. 719 or 720. Ritter, on the contrary, denounces with much indignation the idea that Horace could impute the indecorum of so familiar an intercourse with a freedwoman to a man of the grave occupations and dignified position of Mæcenas, and insists on applying "puella" to Terentia, in which case the poem would be written shortly after the marriage of Mæcenas, which Ritter chooses to date, A.U.C. 725 (*i. e.*, a year after Franke's date for the publication of the Epodes).

CARM. III.

Parentis olim si quis impia manu
   Senile guttur fregerit,
Edit cicutis allium nocentius.
   O dura messorum ilia!
Quid hoc veneni sævit in præcordiis?
   Num viperinus his cruor
Incoctus herbis me fefellit? an malas
   Canidia tractavit dapes?
Ut Argonautas præter omnes candidum*
   Medea mirata est ducem,

---

forma capta est, sic construe, 'non vero Jasonem candidum mirata est præter omnes Argonautas.'"—ORELLI. Macleane prefers the construction which Orelli prohibits, but I like Orelli's the best.

Smeared him with this soul-sickening preparation,
  Which quelled the bulls to the unwonted yoke.
In this she steeped her present to the rival,
  From whom, avenging, soared her dragon-car.
Never such heat from pestilential comets
  Parched dry Apulia, thirsting for a shower;
Less hot that gift which, through the massive shoulders
  Of sturdy Hercules, burned life away.
Jocose Mæcenas, 'tis no laughing matter:
  If e'er thou try it, may thy sweetheart's hand
Ward off thy kiss; and sacred be her refuge
  In the remotest borders of the bed.

EPODE III.

Ignota tauris illigaturum juga
    Perunxit hoc Jasonem;
Hoc delibutis ulta donis pellicem.
    Serpente fugit alite.
Nec tantus unquam siderum insedit vapor
    Siticulosæ Apuliæ,
Nec munus humeris efficacis Herculis
    Inarsit æstuosius.
At, si quid unquam tale concupiveris,
    Jocose Mæcenas, precor
Manum puella savio opponat tuo,
    Extrema et in sponda cubet.

EPODE IV.

AGAINST AN UPSTART.

All the scholiasts agree in considering that the person satirised in this ode was the freedman Menas, lieutenant to Sextus Pompeius, who deserted to Augustus A.U.C. 716. Modern critics have objected to this assumption, and their objections are tersely summed up

As tow'rds the wolf the lamb's inborn repugnance
   Nature makes my antipathy to thee,
Thou on whose flank still burns the Iberian whipcord,*
   Thou on whose limbs still galls the bruise of chains,
Strut as thou wilt in arrogance of purse-pride,
   Fortune can change not the man's native breed.
Mark, as along the Sacred Way ** thou flauntest,
   Puffing thy toga, twice three cubits wide †—
Mark with what frankness indignation loathes thee,
   Seen in the looks of every passer-by ‖ §

---

* "Ibericis funibus." These were cords made of "spartum," usually said to be the Spanish broom. It was made into ropes, especially for ships' rigging. "It may be added, in favour of the theory which makes Menas the hero, that the mention of Spanish ropes seems to imply that the person had suffered on board ship, if not in the country itself, since, as Pliny tells us, ropes of spartum were especially used in ships; and the only way to give point to the epithet is to suppose it had reference to Spain itself, or to the fleet."—MACLEANE.

** The Sacred Way, leading to the Capitol, was the favourite lounge of the idlers.

up and answered by Macleane in his prefatory comment on the ode. In some inscriptions Vedius Rufus has been named instead of Menas. Ritter maintains the accuracy of this identification, and affirms that it was no other than Vedius Pollio, a Roman knight, who had been originally a freedman, mentioned by Seneca, Pliny, and others.—See Ritter's note.

CARM. IV.

Lupis et agnis quanta sortito obtigit,
    Tecum mihi discordia est,
Hibericis peruste funibus* latus,
    Et crura dura compede.
Licet superbus ambules pecunia,
    Fortuna non mutat genus.
Videsne, Sacram metiente te Viam
    Cum bis trium ulnarum toga,†
Ut ora vertat huc et huc euntium
    Liberrima indignatio? §

† "Cum bis trium ulnarum toga." According to Macleane, this applies to the width of the toga, not the length, as commonly translated; I follow his interpretation, but it is disputed.

§ "Ut ora vertat huc et huc euntium
Liberrima indignatio."

I think with Macleane that this appears rather to mean the open indignation which made the passengers turn their looks *towards* him, than turn *away* in disgust, which is the construction of the scholiasts. Yonge suggests a totally different interpretation: "See how a free" (*i.e.*, unreserved, undisguised) "scorn *alters* the *countenance*" (ora vertat) "of all who pass along."

"He, by Triumvirs so inured to lashes,
    As tired the public crier to proclaim,*
Now ploughs some thousand fat Falernian acres,
    And wears the Appian Road out with his nags;
In public shows, despite the law of Otho,†
    He takes a foremost place and sits—a knight.
What boots the equipment of yon floating bulwarks,
    Yon vast array of ponderous brazen prores?
What! against slaves and pirates launch an army, §
    Which has for officer,—that man—that man!"

---

* The Triumviri Capitales had the power of inflicting summary chastisement on slaves. When the scourge was inflicted, a public crier stood by and proclaimed the nature of the crime.

† Fourteen rows in the theatre and amphitheatre, immediately over the orchestra, were by the law of L. Roscius Otho, A. U. C. 686, appropriated to the knights. As the tribunes of the soldiers

'Sectus flagellis hic triumviralibus
  Præconis ad fastidium *
Arat Falerni mille fundi jugera
  Et Appiam mannis terit,
Sedilibusque magnus in primis eques,
  Othone contempto, sedet! †
Quid attinet tot ora navium gravi
  Rostrata duci pondere
Contra latrones atque servilem § manum,
  Hoc, hoc tribuno militum?'

had equestrian rank, if the person satirised were one of them, he could therefore take his seat in one of the fourteen rows, despite the intention of Otho, which was to reserve the front seats for persons of genuine rank.

§ The slaves and pirates are supposed to refer to the fleet of Sextus Pompeius.

EPODE V.

ON THE WITCH CANIDIA.

None of Horace's poems excels this in point of power—and the power herein exhibited is of the highest kind; it is power over the passions of pity and terror. The degree of humour admitted is just sufficient to heighten the effect of the more tragic element. The scene is brought before the eye of the reader with a marvellous distinctness. A boy of good birth, as is shown by the *toga prætexta* and *bulla* which he wears, has been decoyed or stolen from his home, and carried at night to some house—probably Canidia's. The poem opens with his terrified exclamations, as Canidia and her three associate witches stand around him. He is stripped, buried chin-deep in a pit, and tantalised with the sight of food which he is not permitted to taste, till, thus wasted away, his liver and marrow may form the crowning ingredient of the caldron in which the other materials for a philter have been placed. That

"But O,* whatever Power divine in heaven,
   O'er earth and o'er the human race presideth, †
What means this gathering? why on me alone,
   Fixed in fierce stare, those ominous dread faces?

---

* "At, O deorum," &c. The word "at," thus commencing the ode, is significant of the commotion and hurry of the speaker, and also brings the whole scene more vividly before the reader. The poem begins, as it were, in the middle of the boy's address to the witches, omitting what had gone before.

That it is for an old profligate, whom Canidia is resolved to charm back to her, that the philter is prepared, adds to the vileness which the poet ascribes to the hag. This epode was probably composed about the same time as the 8th Satire of the First Book, in which Canidia and Sagana are represented seeking the ghastly materials of their witchcraft, and invoking Hecate and Tisiphone in the Esquilinian burial-ground. The poem has little of the graces of expression which characterise Horace's maturer odes, and in one or two passages the construction is faultily obscure; but the grandeur of the whole conception, and the vigour of the execution, need no comment, and compensate for all defects.

The scholiasts say that Canidia's real name was Gratidia, and that she was a Neapolitan perfume-vender. That she was ever a mistress of Horace's is a conjecture founded upon no evidence, and nothing extant in Horace justifies the assumption. This poem was written when Horace was young, and he could scarcely have remembered, except in his childhood, Canidia more lovely than he invariably represents her.

CARM. V.

'At,* O deorum quidquid in cælo regit †
    Terras et humanum genus!
Quid iste fert tumultus? aut quid omnium
    Voltus in unum me truces?

---

† "Regit," not "regis"—"presides," not "presidest." The boy does not invoke the gods; he is addressing Canidia. It is but a disordered exclamation.

By thine own children, if, indeed, for thee *
    Lucina brought to light true fleshly children—
By this vain purple's childish ornament ***
    By Jove's sure wrath—why are thy looks as deadly
As the stepmother's on the babe she loathes,
    Or wounded wild beast's, glaring on the hunter?"
As the boy pleaded thus, with tremulous lip,
    From him fierce hands rent childhood's robe and bulla,
And naked stood that form which might have moved,
    With its young innocence, a Thracian's pity.

Canidia, all her tangled tresses crisped
    By the contracted folds of angry vipers,
Spake, and bade mandrakes, torn from dead men's
            graves, †
Bade dismal branches of funereal cypress,
And eggs and plumes of the night screech-owl, smeared
    With the toad's loathsome and malignant venom,
Herbs which Iolcos and Hiberia send, ††
    From soils whose richest harvest-crops are poison,
And bones, from jaw of famished wild-bitch snatched, §—
    Bade them all simmer in the Colchian caldron. §§

   * Here he addresses Canidia.
   ** Ritter, Yonge, and Munro have "*adfuit.*"
   *** "Per hoc inane purpurae decus precor." This is the "toga pretexta" which was worn by free Roman children, together with the "bulla," a small round plate of gold suspended from the neck. Both were relinquished on the adoption of the "toga virilis," about the age of fifteen.
   † "Sepulcris caprificos erutas," the wild fig rooted up from graves.
   †† Hiberia here does not, as elsewhere, mean Spain, but a region, now part of Georgia, east of Colchis. Iolcos was a seaport of Thessaly.
   § Why bones snatched from the jaws of a hungry bitch should have the virtue that fits them for ingredients in the witches' caldron

EPODE V.

Per liberos te,* si vocata partubus
    Lucina veris affuit,**
Per hoc inane purpuræ decus precor,***
    Per improbaturum hæc Jovem,
Quid ut noverca me intueris, aut uti
    Petita ferro belua?'
Ut hæc trementi questus ore constitit
    Insignibus raptis puer,
Impube corpus, quale posset impia
    Mollire Thracum pectora;
Canidia, brevibus implicata viperis
    Crines et incomptum caput,
Jubet sepulcris caprificos erutas, †
    Jubet cupressus funebres,
Et uncta turpis ova ranæ sanguine
    Plumamque nocturnæ strigis,
Herbasque, quas Iolcos atque Hiberia ††
    Mittit venenorum ferax,
Et ossa ab ore rapta jejunæ canis, §
    Flammis aduri Colchicis. §§

is not clearly explained by the commentators. It is not only the angry slaver of the famishing bitch robbed of her food that gives the bone its necromantic value—there is virtue in the bone itself. The dog meant is one of the ownerless wild dogs that prowled at night for food, and haunted burial-grounds such as the Esquiline, where the lowest class of the poor were buried so near the surface of the ground that their remains could be easily scratched up, and the bone adapted for the caldron would be a human bone. So, in the "Siege of Corinth"—

    "And he saw the lean dogs beneath the wall
    Hold o'er the dead their carnival,
    Gorging and growling o'er carcass and limb," &c.

§§ "Flammis aduri Colchicis." The materials thus collected by the witches are not burned as fuel in the magic (Colchian) flames, but are boiled as materials for the philter, of which the marrow and liver of the unhappy child are the completing ingredients.

Meanwhile, bare-legged, fell Sagana bedews
  The whole abode with hell-drops from Avernus,*
Her locks erect as some sea-urchin barbed,
  Or wild boar bristling as he runs. Then Veia,
Remorseless crone, loud grunting o'er the toil
  With her fell spade the yawning death-pit hollows,
Wherein they bury the yet living child,
  And twice and thrice each long day mock his famine.†
Chin-deep (as waters on their brim suspend
  The swimmer) plunged, lingering he lives in dying,
To gaze upon the food denied his lips,
  Till the parched liver and the shrivelled marrow
Shall into philters for vile love consume,
  When once, yet staring on the food forbidden,
The glazing eyeballs waste themselves away.
If idle Naples and each neighbouring city
  Rightly believe, the Ariminian hag,
Unnatural Folia, failed not that grim conclave,
  She who could draw the moon and subject stars,
With her Thessalian witch-song, down from heaven.

To them, with thumb-nail pressed to livid tooth,
  Which gnawed and mumbled it, spake dire Canidia.
What said she, or what horror left untold?
  "Ye of my deeds sure arbiters and faithful,
O Night, O Hecate, who o'er silence reign
  In darksome hours to rites mysterious sacred,
Now, now be present; now on hostile homes
  Turn wrath invoked, and demon power revengeful;

---

* From the fount Avernus.
  † "Longo die bis terque mutatae dapis
      Inemori spectaculo."
"Longo" belongs to "die," and not to "spectaculo." "Inemori"

At expedita Sagana, per totam domum
  Spargens Avernales aquas,*
Horret capillis ut marinus asperis
  Echinus, aut currens aper.
Abacta nulla Veia conscientia
  Ligonibus duris humum
Exhauriebat, ingemens laboribus;
  Quo posset infossus puer
Longo die bis terque mutatæ dapis
  Inemori spectaculo; †
Cum promineret ore, quantum exstant aqua
  Suspensa mento corpora;
Exsucta uti medulla et aridum jecur
  Amoris esset poculum,
Interminato cum semel fixæ cibo
  Intabuissent pupulæ.
Non defuisse masculæ libidinis
  Ariminensem Foliam,
Et otiosa credidit Neapolis,
  Et omne vicinum oppidum;
Quæ sidera excantata voce Thessala
  Lunamque cælo deripit.
Hic irresectum sæva dente livido
  Canidia rodens pollicem
Quid dixit aut quid tacuit? 'O rebus meis
  Non infideles arbitræ,
Nox et Diana, quæ silentium regis,
  Arcana cum fiunt sacra,
Nunc, nunc adeste: nunc in hostiles domos
  Iram atque numen vertite!

is not found anywhere else; the ordinary form is "immori."—
MACLEANE.

Now, while amid the horror-breathing woods
  Lurk the wild beasts, couched languid in soft slumber,
Dogs of Subura,* up! bark loud; let all
  Mock the old lecher, with a nard anointed
Than which none subtler could these hands complete.
  But how?† what's this? Have they, then, lost their
    virtue?
The barbarous Medea's direful drugs,
  Wherewith she wreaked her wrongs on that proud
    rival,
Great Creon's daughter, yea, consumed the bride
  By venom steeped into the murderous mantle,
And soared away destroying:—Me, nor herb
  Nor root hath failed to render its dark secrets
Latent in inaccessible ravines.
  The beds he sleeps on are by me besprinkled §
With Lethe of all other loves than mine.
  Ho! ho! yet struts he free,—at large,—protected
By charm of witch more learned than myself.
  Ah, Varus, ah! by no trite hackneyed philters

---

* "Subura," one of the most populous and one of the most profligate streets of Rome. Canidia prays that the barking of the dogs may rouse the street to mock the old man, skulking to other mistresses than herself, and thus scare him back to her. It seems clear from what follows that the nard or unguent was composed by Canidia, though that is disputed by commentators, and the construction itself is obscure. It is this magical unguent that is to cause the dogs to bark—see Orelli's note. Absurdly enough it has been assumed, on the authority of this passage (for what other authority is there?) that Canidia was by profession a vender of perfumes.

† "Quid accidit?" The spell fails—the dogs do not bark. Varus does not go forth into Subura, nor come to Canidia. "Do the drugs of Medea fail?" &c. "She speaks," says Macleane, "as if she had been actually using the drugs of Medea."

Formidolosis dum latent silvis feræ,
  Dulci sopore languidæ,
Senem, quod omnes rideant, adulterum
  Latrent Suburanæ * canes
Nardo perunctum, quale non perfectius
  Meæ laborarint manus.—
Quid accidit? † Cur dira barbaræ minus
  Venena Medeæ valent,
Quibus superbam fugit ulta pellicem,
  Magni Creontis filiam,
Cum palla, tabo munus imbutum, novam
  Incendio nuptam abstulit?
Atqui nec herba, nec latens in asperis
  Radix fefellit me locis.
Indormit unctis omnium cubilibus
  Oblivione pellicum. §—
Ah! ah! solutus ambulat veneficæ
  Scientioris carmine.
Non usitatis, Vare, potionibus,
  O multa fleturum caput,

§ "Indormit unctis omnium cubilibus
    Oblivione pellicum."

The sense of this passage is exceedingly obscure, and has been subjected to various interpretations. I adopt that of Orelli, viz.—Canidia had smeared the couch on which Varus slept with drugs to make him forgetful of all women but herself; taking "unctis" with "oblivione," anointed with oblivion—"omnium pellicum," "of all wantons." Still the construction is not satisfactory, because, just before, Canidia supposes that Varus was out on his rambles, from which the barking dogs were to scare him to her, and she is surprised to find that he is quietly asleep.

Ill-fated wretch, shalt thou rush back to me,
　Thy truant heart no Marsian charms recover *—
A mightier spell I weave; a direr bowl
　Now will I brim, to tame thy scornful bosom.
Sooner the sky shall sink below the sea,
　And over both the earth shall be extended,
Than thou not burn for me, as in the smoke
　Of these black flames now burns this dull bitumen."
Then the child spoke, not seeking, as before,
　Those impious hell-hags with mild words to soften,
But pausing long, now in his last despair,
　Launched the full wrath of Thyestëan curses. †
"Witchcraft invert not the great laws divine
　Of right and wrong as they invert things human; §

---

* "Ad me recurres; nec vocata mens tua
　　　Marsis redibit vocibus."

The Marsian witchcrafts were those in vogue with the populace. The sense is not, as commonly translated, that his mind or reason (mens), maddened by Canidia's spell, shall not be restored to him by the countercharms of the Marsian witchcraft; but that he shall run back to her, and that his mind or heart will not be thus restored to her by her employment of any common vulgar incantations. No, she is now preparing a mightier bowl (referring to the victim present), &c.

† "Thyesteas preces." Curses such as Thyestes might have invoked on Atreus, who slaughtered and served up at the banquet his brother's children.

§ "Venena magnum fas nefasque non valent
　　Convertere humanam vicem;
　Diris agam vos."

Of all the obscure passages in the poem this is the most obscure. The contradictory interpretations of various commentators have not served to render it less so. The translation most in vogue is that suggested by Lambinus: "Witchcraft (venena) can invert the great principle of wrong and right, but cannot invert the condition

Ad me recurres; nec vocata mens tua
  Marsis redibit vocibus: *
Majus parabo, majus infundam tibi
  Fastidienti poculum.
Priusque cælum sidet inferius mari,
  Tellure porrecta super,
Quam non amore sic meo flagres, uti
  Bitumen atris ignibus.'—
Sub hæc puer, jam non, ut ante, mollibus
  Lenire verbis impias;
Sed dubius unde rumperet silentium,
  Misit Thyesteas preces: †
'Venena magnum fas nefasque non valent
  Convertere humanam vicem;
Diris agam vos; § dira detestatio
  Nulla expiatur victima.

or fate (or vicissitude in the fate) of men," "valent" being understood in the first clause. Munro, Introduction, p. xxvIII, adopts the arrangement of Lambinus, with one point of difference. "I do not think," he says, "'Magnum' can be joined with 'fas nefasque.' I have therefore made it parenthetical where it seems to me to have much force. The meaning is, 'venena (id quod magnum est) fas nefasque valent Convertere, humanam vicem non valent.'" Ritter takes "venena" as poisons which may be beneficial as medicaments, or deadly, used with malignant purposes, and are thus "magnum fas nefasque;" and takes "humanam vicem" as the retribution due to human deeds. Orelli, in an excursus, gives, with his usual candour, not less than nine various interpretations, but very decidedly pronounces himself in favour of that which I believe he originates, and which is certainly a bold one. He assumes "magnum fas nefasque" to be the subject, and that the sense is, "the great law of wrong and right (divinæ leges), according to human sense (humanam vicem), cannot convert (soften and bend) witchcraft or the hearts of witches." Macleane says, I think correctly, "that if this view of the construction were adopted, it would be better to render 'humanam vicem' 'on behalf of men or of humanity.'" Mac-

So to those laws my dooming curse appeals,
  And draws down wrath too dire for expiation.
Mark where thus foully murdered I expire,
  With every night I haunt you as a Fury,*
Mangle your cheeks, a ghost with bird-like claws;
  For such the power of those dread gods the Manes.
On your unquiet bosoms I shall sit
  An incubus, and murder sleep with horror;
And at the last, as through the streets ye slink,
  Street after street the crowd shall rise against you,
Hither and thither hounded, till to death
  Stoned by fierce mobs, vile hags obscene, ye perish;
By wolves and Esquilinian birds of prey
  Your limbs unburied shall be rent and scattered.
Nor shall my parents, who alas! survive
  To mourn me, lose this spectacle of vengeance."

Ieane suggests two other interpretations (see his note), which appear to me more open to objection. Yonge, following Orelli in the main points, asks whether it may not be better to reverse the order, and take "venena" for the nominative case—thus, "sorceries (and those who use them) cannot change (*i.e.*, turn aside or defeat) the divine law, as they can men and men's law; therefore I appeal to them: such an appeal will draw down a wrath implacable." He renders "humanam vicem" "in human fashion," "after the manner of men." I have adopted the sense of this interpretation.

Quin, ubi perire jussus exspiravero,
　　Nocturnus occurram Furor,*
Petamque voltus umbra curvis unguibus,
　　Quæ vis deorum est Manium;
Et inquietis assidens præcordiis,
　　Pavore somnos auferam.
Vos turba vicatim hinc et hinc saxis petens
　　Contundet obscœnas anus;
Post insepulta membra different lupi
　　Et Esquilinæ alites;
Neque hoc parentes, heu mihi superstites,
　　Effugerit spectaculum.'

Witchcrafts is a better word here than sorceries, which properly signify divination by lot. Two other interpretations have been suggested to me by eminent scholars: 1st, Witchcraft cannot distort (or overthrow) the great rules of right and wrong in the interest of men (taking "humanam vicem" in the sense, "hominum causa"). 2d, Witchcraft cannot overthrow the great law of wrong and right —human retribution.

* "Furor"—literally, "a personified madness."

EPODE VI.

AGAINST CASSIUS.

It is by no means clear who is the unlucky object of these verses. Acron says he was a satirical poet of the name of Cassius, upon the strength of which the scholiast in Cruquius assumes him to have been the not uncelebrated orator Cassius Severus, who was banished by Augustus, and died in poverty and exile about sixty-three years after the date of this ode. This supposition is not tenable, for Cassius Severus, as Orelli remarks, must have been a boy, or a youth of

Why snap at the guests who do nobody harm,
   Turning tail at the sight of a wolf?
O curl thy vain threats why not venture on me,
   Who can give back a bite for a bite?
Like mastiff Molossian or Sparta's dun hound,
   Kindly friend to the shepherd am I;
But I prick up my ears, and away through the snows,
   If a wild beast of prey run before;
But thou, if thou fillest the woods with thy bark,
   Art struck dumb at the sniff of a bone.
Ah, beware! I am rough when I come upon knaves,
   Ah, beware of a toss from my horns!
I'm as sharp as the wit whom Lycambes deceived,
   Or the bitter foe Bupalus roused;*
Dost thou think, when a cur shows the grin of his teeth,
   That I'll weep, unavenged, like a child?

---

* Archilochus, to whom Lycambes refused his daughter Neobule, after having first promised her to him. The poet avenged himself in verses so stinging, that Lycambes is said to have hanged himself. Bupalus was a sculptor, who, with his brother artist

of about twenty, when the ode was composed; nor is there any authority on record that Cassius Severus was a poet. Other commentators have supposed the person meant was Mævius or Bavius. If the right name be Cassius, nothing is known about him; nor is it of any importance. Horace's invective, for what we know to the contrary, might have been as unjust and inappropriate as the lampoons of irritable young poets generally are. Ritter conjectures the person there satirised to have been Furius Bibaculus, notorious for the bitterness of his iambics, and who included Octavian Cæsar in his attacks.

CARM. VI.

Quid immerentes hospites vexas, canis,
    Ignavus adversum lupos?
Quin huc inanes, si potes, vertis minas,
    Et me remorsurum petis?
Nam, qualis aut Molossus, aut fulvus Lacon,
    Amica vis pastoribus,
Agam per altas aure sublata nives,
    Quæcunque præcedet fera:
Tu, cum timenda voce complesti nemus,
    Projectum odoraris cibum.
Cave, cave: namque in malos asperrimus
    Parata tollo cornua;
Qualis Lycambæ spretus infido gener,
    Aut acer hostis Bupalo.*
An, si quis atro dente me petiverit,
    Inultus ut flebo puer?

Athenis, ridiculed or caricatured the uncomely features of Hipponax, and his verses are said (though not truly) to have had the same fatal effect on the sculptor that those of Archilochus had upon Lycambes.

EPODE VII.

TO THE ROMANS.

This poem is referred by Orelli (who rightly considers it composed at a comparatively early age) to the beginning of the war of Perusia, A.U.C. 713-14, to which period the 16th Epode is ascribed. Others refer it to A.U.C. 716, the expedition of Augustus against

O guilty! whither, whither would ye run?
  Why swords just sheathed to those right hands refitted?
Is there too little of the Latian blood
  Shed on the land or wasted on the ocean,
Not that the Roman may consign to flames
  The haughty battlements of envious Carthage;
Not that the intact Briton may be seen
  In captive chains the Sacred Slope descending;
But that, compliant to the Parthian's prayer,
  By her own right hand this great Rome shall perish?
Not so with wolves; lions not lions rend;
  The wild beast preys not on his own wild kindred.
Is it blind frenzy, or some demon Power,*
  Or wilful crime that hurries you thus headlong?
Reply! All silent; pallor on all cheeks,
  And on all minds dumb conscience-stricken stupor.
So is it then! so rest on Roman heads
  Doom, and the guilt of fratricidal murder,
Ever since† Remus shed upon this soil
  The innocent blood atoned for by descendants.

---

* "Vis acrior," "a fatal necessity;" equivalent to θεοῦ βίαν.
—ORELLI, MACLEANE.

against Sextus Pompeius, which is not very probable; others, again, including Franke, to the much later date of 722, the last war between Augustus and Mark Antony. Ritter contends that it relates to the war against Brutus and Cassius.

Carm. VII.

Quo, quo scelesti ruitis? aut cur dexteris
    Aptantur enses conditi?
Parumne campis atque Neptuno super
    Fusum est Latini sanguinis,
Non, ut superbas invidæ Carthaginis
    Romanus arces ureret;
Intactus aut Britannus ut descenderet
    Sacra catenatus Via,
Sed ut, secundum vota Parthorum, sua
    Urbs hæc periret dextera?
Neque hic lupis mos, nec fuit leonibus
    Unquam, nisi in dispar, feris.
Furorne cæcus, an rapit vis acrior?*
    An culpa? Responsum date!
Tacent; et albus ora pallor inficit,
    Mentesque perculsæ stupent.
Sic est: acerba fata Romanos agunt,
    Scelusque fraternæ necis,
Ut† immerentis fluxit in terram Remi
    Sacer nepotibus cruor.

† "Ut immerentis," &c. "Ut" here has the signification of "ex quo," ever since.—Orelli, Macleane.

Epode VIII. Omitted.

EPODE IX.

To Mæcenas.

The date of this ode is not to be mistaken. It "was written when the news of Actium was fresh, in September A.U.C. 723. It was addressed to Mæcenas, and it is impossible to read it and suppose he had just arrived from Actium, where some will have it he was engaged."—MACLEANE.

The fine ode, Book I. 37, "Nunc est bibendum," was written a year later, after the news of the taking of Alexandria and the death of Cleopatra. In both these odes it will be observable that Horace avoids naming Mark Antony—some say from his friendship
to

When (may Jove grant it!) shall I quaff with thee
   Under thy lofty dome, my glad Mæcenas,*
Cups of that Cæcuban reserved for feasts—
   Quaff in rejoicing for victorious Cæsar,
While with the hymn symphonious music swells—
   Here Dorian lyre, there Phrygian fifes commingling?
As late we feasted, when from ocean chased,
   The Son of Neptune fled his burning navies,†
He who did threaten to impose on Rome
   That which he took from slaves, his friends—the fetter.

---

* "Beate Mæcenas." The epithet "beate" seems here to apply to the gladness of Mæcenas at the good news, rather than to his general opulence or felicitous fortunes.

† "Neptunius dux," Sextus Pompeius, who boasted himself to be the Son of Neptune. Though Horace speaks of the rejoicing

to the Triumvir's son Iulus, to whom he addresses Ode II. Lib. IV.; but at the battle of Actium Iulus was a mere boy, and it is not possible to conceive how Horace was even acquainted with him at that time. There must have been some other reason for this reticence, and it is quite as likely to have been one of artistic taste as one founded on personal or political considerations; for Horace does not mention by name Cleopatra, nor even Sextus Pompeius. It is consistent with the dignity of lyric song to avoid the direct mention of the name of our national enemy, especially if conquered. In an English lyrical poem on the Crimean war, we should scarcely think it strange if the poet did not obtrude on us the name of Nicholas.

CARM. IX.

Quando repostum Cæcubum ad festas dapes,
    Victore lætus Cæsare,
Tecum sub alta, sic Jovi gratum, domo,
    Beate Mæcenas,* bibam,
Sonante mixtum tibiis carmen lyra,
    Hac Dorium, illis barbarum?
Ut nuper, actus cum freto Neptunius
    Dux† fugit, ustis navibus,
Minatus Urbi vincla, quæ detraxerat
    Servis amicus perfidis.

at the defeat of Sextus Pompeius as if it were of late ("ut nuper"), it occurred between five and six years before (A.U.C. 718). Fugitive slaves formed a large part of the force of Sextus Pompeius.

A Roman (ah! deny it after times),*
 Sold into bondage to a female master,
Empales her camp-works,** and parades her arms,
 And serves, her soldier, under wrinkled eunuchs.
Shaming war's standards, in their midst, the sun
 Beholds a tent lawn-draped against mosquitoes.†
Hitherwards,†† then, Gaul's manly riders wheeled
 Two thousand fretting steeds, and shouted "Cæsar."
And all along the hostile fleet swift prores
 Backed from the fight, and slunk into the haven.§
Hail, God of Triumph! why delay so long
 The golden cars and sacrificial heifers?
Hail, God of Triumph! from Jugurthine wars
 Thou brought'st not back to Rome an equal chieftain;
Not Africanus,§§ to whom Valour built
 A sepulchre on ground which once was Carthage.
Routed by sea, by land, the Foe hath changed
 For weeds of mourning his imperial purple;
Or spreading sails to unpropitious winds
 For Crete, ennobled by her hundred cities;

---

 * This does not refer to Mark Antony himself, but to the Roman soldiers under him. The singular number is used poetically.

 ** "Fert vallum." The Roman soldier carried palisades ("vallum") for an empaled camp.

 † "Conopium." The mosquito net or curtain in use in Egypt, and still common in Italy and hot climates, placed in the midst of the "signa militaria"—*i.e.*, the rising ground on which the military standards were grouped round the prætorium or imperial tent.

 †† "At huc." The reading in the MSS. varies. Orelli has "at hoc," and takes "hoc" with "frementes Galli." I prefer Macleane's reading, "at huc," taking "frementes" with "equos;" "huc" thus means "hither," "to our side." Ritter has "ad hunc," contending that "ad" has the force of "adversus"—*i.e.*, against Antonius, who is signified, though not named. Munro

Romanus,* eheu, posteri negabitis,
  Emancipatus feminæ,
Fert vallum** et arma miles, et spadonibus
  Servire rugosis potest,
Interque signa turpe militaria
  Sol adspicit conopium.†
At huc †† frementes verterunt bis mille equos
  Galli, canentes Cæsarem,
Hostiliumque navium portu latent
  Puppes sinistrorsum citæ.§
Io Triumphe, tu moraris aureos
  Currus, et intactas boves?
Io Triumphe, nec Jugurthino parem
  Bello reportasti ducem,
Neque Africanum,§§ cui super Carthaginem
  Virtus sepulcrum condidit.
Terra marique victus hostis punico
  Lugubre mutavit sagum;
Aut ille centum nobilem Cretam urbibus,
  Ventis iturus non suis,

has also "ad hunc," observing that "it has most authority; but what Horace did here write it is impossible to say. 'Ad hunc' may = 'ad solem.'" As the line refers to the desertion to Cæsar of the Gauls, or cavalry of Galatia, under their king Deiotarus, "at huc" seems the simplest interpretation.

§ "Hostiliumque navium portu latent
    Puppes sinistrorsum citæ."

Macleane considers the meaning of the words impenetrably obscure, from our ignorance of the Roman nautical phrases. He inclines to favour Bentley's supposition, that "sinistrorsum citæ" may be equivalent to πρύμνην κρούεσθαι, "to back water;" adding, "something of that sort, connected with flight, I have no doubt it means."

§§ "Neque Africanum," not, as some would have it, "Africano," as referring to the African war.

Or by the south blast dashed on Afric's sands,
  Or, drifting shoreless, lost in doubtful seas.

Ho there, good fellow! out with larger bowls,
  And delicate Chian wines, or those of Lesbos;
Or rather, mix us lusty Cæcuban,
  A juice austere, which puts restraint on sickness;
The Care-Unbinder well may free us now
  From every doubt that fortune smiles on Cæsar.

Exercitatas aut petit Syrtes Noto,
  Aut fertur incerto mari.
Capaciores affer huc, puer, scyphos,
  Et Chia vina aut Lesbia.
Vel, quod fluentem nauseam coërceat,
  Metire nobis Cæcubum:
Curam metumque Cæsaris rerum juvat
  Dulci Lyæo solvere.

EPODE X.

ON MÆVIUS SETTING OUT ON A VOYAGE.

The name of Mævius has become proverbially identified with the ideal of a bad poet; but, after all, the justice of this very unpleasant immortality rests upon no satisfactory evidence. Virgil, with laconic disdain, dismisses him and Bavius to obloquy, and this poem is a specimen of Horace's mode, in his hot youth, of treating a person to whom he owed a grudge. But poets are very untrustworthy judges of the merits of a contemporary poet, whom, for some reason or other, they dislike. If nothing of Southey be left to remote posterity, and he is only then to be judged by what Byron has said of him, Southey would appear a sort of Mævius. On the other hand, what would Byron seem if nothing were left of his works, and, one or two thousand years hence, he were to be judged by the opinions of his verse which Southey and Wordsworth and Coleridge have left on record? As to the severest things said of Mævius by writers of a later generation, and who had probably never read a line of him, they are but echoes of the old lampoons, "Give a dog a bad name," &c. If it be true, as the commentator in Cruquius says, that Mævius was "a detractor of all learned men," and a cultivator of archaisms, or an elder school of expression, "sectator vocum

Under ill-boding auspices puts forth the vessel
 Which has Mævius—a rank-smelling cargo—on board;
Either side of that vessel, with surges the roughest,
 O be mindful, I pray thee, wild Auster, to scourge!

vocum antiquarum," it is probable enough that he incurred the resentment of Horace and the scorn of Virgil by his attacks on their modern style, and that his adherence to the elder forms of Latin poetry was uncongenial to their own taste. For Virgil's contemptuous mention, indeed, there might be some cause less general, if Mævius and Bavius wrote the Anti-Bucolica ascribed to them—*i. e.*, two pastorals in parody of the Eclogues; and especially if Mævius were the author of a very ready and a very witty attempt to turn him into ridicule. Virgil, reciting the First Book of his Georgics, after the words, "Nudus ara, sere nudus," came to a dead halt, when some one, said to be either Mævius or Bavius, finished the line by calling out, "habebis frigore febrem." Whoever made that joke must have been clever enough to be a disagreeable antagonist. One thing, at all events, seems pretty evident—viz., that Mævius must have had power of some kind to excite the muse of Horace to so angry an excess. Had he been a man wholly without mark or following, he could scarcely have stung to such wrath even a youthful poet. Be that as it may, this ode has all the vigour of a good hater, and there is much of the gusto of true humour in its extravagance. The exact date of its composition is unknown, but it bears the trace of very early youth. Grotefend assigns it to A.U.C. 716, when Horace was twenty-seven.

CARM. X.

Mala soluta navis exit alite,
    Ferens olentem Mævium:
Ut horridis utrumque verberes latus,
    Auster, memento fluctibus!

On an ocean upheaved from its inmost foundations,
  May the dark frowning Eurus snap cables and oars;
And may Aquilo rise in his might as when rending
  Upon hill-peaks the holm-oaks that rock to his blast!
On the blackness of night let no friendly star glimmer
  Save the baleful Orion, whose setting is storm;
Nor the deep know a billow more calm than the breakers
  Which o'erwhelmed the victorious armada of Greece,
When, from Ilion consumed, to the vessel of Ajax
  Pallas* turned the wrath due to her temple profaned!
Ha, what sweat-drops will run from the brows of thy sailors,
  And how palely thy puddle-blood ooze from thy cheeks;
As thou call'st out for aid—with that shriek which shames manhood†—
  On the Jove who disdains such a caitiff to hear;
When thy keel strains and cracks in the deep gulf Ionic,
  Howling back the grim howl of the stormy south-blast.
But O! if in some desolate creek thou shalt furnish
  To the maw of the sea-gulls a banquet superb,
To the Tempests a lamb and lewd goat shall be offered
  As a tribute of thanks for deliverance from thee.

---

* It is cleverly said by one of the critics, that Pallas is appropriately enough referred to here as the avenger of the bad poetry with which Mævius had insulted her.

Niger rudentes Eurus, inverso mari,
    Fractosque remos differat;
Insurgat Aquilo, quantus altis montibus
    Frangit trementes ilices;
Nec sidus atra nocte amicum appareat,
    Qua tristis Orion cadit;
Quietiore nec feratur æquore,
    Quam Graia victorum manus,
Cum Pallas* usto vertit iram ab Ilio
    In impiam Ajacis ratem!
O quantus instat navitis sudor tuis,
    Tibique pallor luteus,
Et illa non virilis ejulatio,†
    Preces et aversum ad Jovem,
Ionius udo cum remugiens sinus
    Noto carinam ruperit!
Opima quod si præda curvo litore
    Porrecta mergos juveris,
Libidinosus immolabitur caper
    Et agna Tempestatibus.

† "*Illa* non virilis ejulatio." He speaks as though he heard the man crying.—MACLEANE.

EPODES XI. AND XII. OMITTED.

EPODE XIII.

TO FRIENDS.

Of all the Epodes, this, of which the metre consists of a hexameter verse, with one made up of a dimeter iambic and half a pentameter, appears to have most of the lyrical spirit and character of the Odes. The poem, addressed to a party of friends in winter, suggests comparison with the 9th Ode of the First Book, "Vides, ut alta stet nive candidum," also a winter song; but the occasion is very different, and the spirit that pervades it not less so. Ode ix. Lib. I. has no reference to public troubles; unless, indeed, a reader should indorse the very far-fetched supposition that verse 7, "Permitte divis cætera," has a political allusion. Its main image is in the picture of an individual, and the happy mode in which, while yet young, that individual may pass his day. Its tone is cheerful, and with no insinuation of pathos. This epode, on the other hand, is evidently addressed to friends excited by anxieties and apprehensions in common. If it be allowable to draw a conjecture from the touching illustration of the fate of Achilles, doomed in the land of Assaracus to a stormy life and an early death, the poem might have been written between the date of Horace's departure
into

Frowning storm has contracted the face of the heaven,
   Rains and snows draw the upper air heavily down;
Now the sea, now the forests, resound with the roar
   Of wild Aquilo rushing from hill-tops on Thrace.

into Asia Minor, in the service of Brutus, and that of the trials and dangers which closed at the field of Philippi, A.U.C. 712. Ritter, indeed, places its date in the interval between the death of Cassius and the battle of Philippi. It may, however, be observed, that if the invitation to the feastmaster to bring forth the wine stored in the consulship of Torquatus is to be taken literally, wine of that age could scarcely have been found in the commissariat of Brutus. If not written while in the camp of Brutus, it was probably composed between A. U. C. 712 and 716, soon after Horace's return to Rome, before the fortunes of his life, and perhaps his political views, were changed by the favour of Mæcenas, and while his chief associates would naturally have been among the remnants of the party with whom he had fought, and to whose minds (if there be anything peculiarly appropriate in the reference to Achilles) military dangers in a foreign land might still be the salient apprehension. It is evidently written some years before Ode IX. Lib. I. Horace here classes himself emphatically with the young. In Ode IX. he addresses Thaliarchus, or the feastmaster, with the half-envious sentiment of a man who points out the pleasures of youth to another—who yet sympathises with those pleasures, but is somewhat receding from them himself.

Carm. XIII.

Horrida tempestas cælum contraxit, et imbres
    Nivesque deducunt Jovem; nunc mare, nunc siluæ
Threïcio Aquilone sonant: rapiamus, amici,
    Occasionem de die, dumque virent genua,

Seize, my friends, on To-day—foul or fair it is ours—
  While yet firm are the knees, nor unseemly is joy;
And let Gravity loosen his hold on the brows *
  Which he now overcasts with the cloud of his scowl.
Broach the cask which was born with myself in the
      year
  Of the Consul Torquatus.** All else be unsaid;
For, perchance, by some turn in our fortunes, a god
  May all else to their place in times brighter restore.
Now let nard Achæmenian afford us its balm;
  Doubt and dread let the chords of Cyllene † dispel;
Listen all to the song which the Centaur renowned
  Sang of old to the ears of his great foster-son:—
"Boy invincible, goddess-born, mortal thyself, ††
  The domain of Assaracus waits thee afar;
There the petty § Scamander's cold streams cut their way,
  And there slidingly lapses the smooth Simoïs.
From that land, by the certain decree of their woof,
  Have the Weavers of Doom broken off thy return,
And thy mother, the blue-eyed, shall never again
  Bear thee back o'er the path of her seas to thy home.
But when there, let each burden of evils ordained,
  From thy bosom be lifted by wine and by song;
Soothers they of a converse so sweet, it can charm
  All the cares which deform our existence away."

---

* "Obducta solvatur fronte senectus." "Obducta," as if clouded with care and sadness.—ORELLI. Orelli interprets "senectus" in the sense of "morositas," "tædium," to which the word "senium" is more frequently applied. Macleane renders it "melancholy," in which sense, however, he allows it is used nowhere else. I think the right meaning is "gravity" or "austerity," in which sense it is employed by Cicero, De Clar. Orat. 76, "Plena litteratæ senectutis oratio."

Et decet, obducta solvatur fronte senectus.*
 Tu vina Torquato move Consule pressa meo.**
Cetera mitte loqui: deus hæc fortasse benigna
 Reducet in sedem vice. Nunc et Achæmenio
Perfundi nardo juvat, et fide Cyllenea †
 Levare diris pectora sollicitudinibus;
Nobilis ut grandi cecinit Centaurus alumno:
 'Invicte, mortalis dea nate puer Thetide, ††
Te manet Assaraci tellus, quam frigida parvi §
 Findunt Scamandri flumina lubricus et Simoïs,
Unde tibi reditum certo subtemine Parcæ
 Rupere; nec mater domum cærula te revehet.
Illic omne malum vino cantuque levato,
 Deformis ægrimoniæ dulcibus alloquiis.'

** "Tu vina Torquato," &c. Here he addresses himself to the master of the feast. Sextus Manlius Torquatus was consul A. U. C. 689, the year of Horace's birth—"O nata mecum consule Manlio," Lib. III. xxi., 1.

† "Fide Cyllenea,"—viz., the lyre, invented by Mercury, born on Mount Cyllene, in Arcadia. There seems to me much beauty in the choice of the word, which introduces an image of Arcadian freedom from care—the ideal holiday life.

†† Achilles.

§ Ritter supposes that the Scamander is here emphatically called small (parvi Scamandri flumina) antithetically to "grandi alumno"—the great hero who found the scene of his actions by a stream so small. Should this conjecture, exquisitely critical, if not too refined, be admitted, then "lubricus et Simoïs" must form a part of the antithesis insinuated; *i.e.*, actions so great beside a stream so small—actions so vehement and of renown so loud, beside a stream so smooth.

EPODE XIV.

TO MÆCENAS IN EXCUSE FOR INDOLENCE IN COMPLETING THE VERSES HE HAD PROMISED.

It is impossible to say whether the verses thus promised and deferred were, as commonly supposed, the collection composed in this Book of Epodes, or some single iambic poem. The context seems to favour

Why this soft sloth, through inmost sense diffusing
    Oblivion as complete'
As if with parched lip I had drained from Lethe
    Whole beakers brimmed with sleep?—
Thou kill'st me with that question oft-repeated—
    Mæcenas, truthful man,*
A song I promised thee; to keep my promise
    A god, a god forbids—
Forbids the iambics, for I have begun them,
    To shape themselves to close.†
Thus it is said, by love inflamed, the Teian
    Lost his diviner art:
And on the shell to which he wailed his sorrow,
    Music imperfect died.
Thou too art scorched; enjoy thy lot; no fairer
    Flame, shot from Helen's eyes,
Fired Troy:—me Phryne burns—a wench too glowing
    To stint her warmth to one.

---

* "Candide Mæcenas." "Candide" here has the signification of honourable or truthful. You kill me—you, a man of honour—asking me so often why I do not fulfil my promise.

favour the latter supposition. The beauty who inflames Mæcenas, so gracefully mentioned at the close of the poem, is, according to the scholiasts, certainly Terentia, whom Mæcenas was then either married to or courting. And that assumption is generally adopted by modern critics. Still it scarcely seems consistent with Roman manners, or with Horace's good breeding and knowledge of the world, that he should imply a comparison between his passing caprice for a public wanton, and the honourable love of a man of the highest station to the lady he had married, or was wooing in marriage.

Carm. XIV.

Mollis inertia cur tantam diffuderit imis
    Oblivionem sensibus,
Pocula Lethæos ut si ducentia somnos
    Arente fauce traxerim,
Candide Mæcenas,* occidis sæpe rogando:
    Deus, deus nam me vetat
Inceptos, olim promissum carmen, iambos
    Ad umbilicum adducere.†
Non aliter Samio dicunt arsisse Bathyllo
    Anacreonta Teïum,
Qui persæpe cava testudine flevit amorem,
    Non elaboratum ad pedem.
Ureris ipse miser: quod si non pulchrior ignis
    Accendit obsessam Ilion,
Gaude sorte tua; me libertina, neque uno
    Contenta, Phryne macerat.

† "Ad umbilicum adducere," is to bring a volume to the last sheet.—Macleane.

EPODE XV.

TO NEÆRA.

This poem may have been an imitation of the Greek, but as Horace pointedly introduces his own name

'Twas night—the moon shone forth in cloudless heaven
    Amid the lesser stars,
When thou didst mock, in vows myself had taught thee,
    The great presiding gods;
Closer than round the ilex clings the ivy,
    Clasping me with twined arms:
"Long as the wolf shall prey upon the sheepfold—
    Long as the seaman's foe,
Baleful Orion, rouse the wintry billows—
    Or the caressing breeze
Ripple the unshorn ringlets of Apollo,
    Our mutual love shall be!"
Ah! thou shalt mourn to find me firm, Neæra;
    For if in Flaccus aught
Of man be left, he brooks not halved embraces;
    Stooped to no second rank,
His love shall leave thee, and explore its equal.
    The heart, in which the pang
Of the last treason once makes sure its entry,
    Is ever henceforth proof
To charms which perfidy has rendered hateful.
    And thou, O happier one!
Whoe'er thou art, in my defeat exulting,
    Be rich in herds and lands;

name as that of the complainant, it must be inferred that, at all events, he meant to be understood as speaking in his own person. The probability is in favour of the supposition that it was the expression of a genuine sentiment, and addressed to a real person. Macleane pushes too far his sceptical theory that Horace's love-poems are merely artistic exercises, like those of Cowley.

Carm. XV.

Nox erat, et cælo fulgebat Luna sereno
    Inter minora sidera,
Cum tu, magnorum numen læsura deorum,
    In verba jurabas mea,
Artius atque hedera procera adstringitur ilex,
    Lentis adhærens brachiis:
Dum pecori lupus, et nautis infestus Orion
    Turbaret hibernum mare,
Intonsosque agitaret Apollinis aura capillos,
    Fore hunc amorem mutuum.
O dolitura mea multum virtute Neæra!
    Nam, si quid in Flacco viri est,
Non feret assiduas potiori te dare noctes,
    Et quæret iratus parem,
Nec semel offensæ cedet constantia formæ,
    Si certus intrarit dolor.
Et tu, quicunque es felicior atque meo nunc
    Superbus incedis malo,

And as for gold, I give thee all Pactolus;
  Know all the lore occult
Stored by Pythagoras re-born; in beauty
  Nireus himself excel;
And yet, alas! in store for thee my sorrow,
  Thou too wilt mourn
Loves with such ease made over to another—
  My turn for mockery then!

Sis pecore et multa dives tellure licebit,
  Tibique Pactolus fluat,
Nec te Pythagoræ fallant arcana renati,
  Formaque vincas Nirea;
Eheu! translatos alio mærebis amores:
  Ast ego vicissim risero.

EPODE XVI.

TO THE ROMAN PEOPLE (OR RATHER TO HIS OWN POLITICAL FRIENDS).

This poem is generally supposed to have been composed at the commencement of the Perusian war, A.U.C. 713—the year following the battle of Philippi, when the state of Italy was indeed deplorable, and the fortunes of Horace himself at the worst. He had forfeited

Another age worn out in civil wars,*
   And Rome sinks weighed down by her own sheer forces,
Whom nor the bordering Marsians could destroy;
   Nor Porsena, threatening with Etruscan armies;
Nor rival Capua,** nor fierce Spartacus,
   Nor Allobroge † in all revolts a traitor;
Nor fierce Germania's blue-eyed giant sons;
   Nor Hannibal, abhorred by Roman mothers,§—
That is the Rome which we, this race, destroy;
   We, impious victims by ourselves devoted,
And to the wild beast and the wilderness
   Restoring soil which Romans called their country.

---

* "Altera ætas," the preceding age being that of Sulla.
** "Æmula nec virtus Capuæ." Capua, after the battle of Cannæ, aspired to the 'imperium' of Italy.—Liv. 23, 2.
† "Novisque rebus infidelis Allobrox." This line is generally supposed to refer to the Allobrogian ambassadors, who, at the time of Catiline's conspiracy, promised to aid it, but afterwards betrayed the conspirators, and became the chief witnesses against them. The Allobroges, a Gallic people on the left bank of the Rhone, two years later broke out in war, and, invading Gallia Narbonensis,

feited his patrimony, and it was two years before he was even introduced to Mæcenas. At that time he would have been twenty-four. The poem has the character of youth in its defects and its beauties. The redundance of its descriptive passages is in marked contrast to the terseness of description which Horace studies in his odes; and there is something declamatory in its general tone which is at variance with the simpler utterance of lyrical art. On the other hand, it has all the warmth of genuine passion; and in sheer vigour of composition Horace has rarely excelled it.

CARM. XVI.

Altera jam teritur bellis civilibus ætas, ^a
  Suis et ipsa Roma viribus ruit:
Quam neque finitimi valuerunt perdere Marsi,
  Minacis aut Etrusca Porsenæ manus,
Æmula nec virtus Capuæ,** nec Spartacus acer,
  Novisque rebus infidelis Allobrox, †
Nec fera cærulea domuit Germania pube,
  Parentibusque abominatus Hannibal, §
Impia perdemus devoti sanguinis ætas,
  Ferisque rursus occupabitur solum.

were defeated by the governor of that province, C. Pomptinius. The line may, however, be intended to designate the general character of this people, without any special reference to the conduct of their ambassadors in the conspiracy of Catiline.

§ "Parentibusque abominatus Hannibal." Orelli and Dillenburger interpret "parentibus" as "our fathers," "the former generation." Doering, Ritter, and Macleane, interpret the word in the sense of "bella matribus detestata," c. i. 1, 24, in which latter sense the line is translated.

Woe! on the ashes of Imperial Rome
  Shall the barbarian halt his march, a victor;
And the wild horseman with a clanging hoof
  Trample the site which was the world's great city,
And—horrid sight—in scorn to winds and sun
  Scatter the shrouded bones of Rome's first founder.*
If haply all, or those amongst you all,
  Who be of nobler nature, ask for counsel
How to escape the endurance of such ills,
  I know none better than this old example:
Leaving their lands, their Lares, and their shrines,
  To wolf and wild boar, went forth the Phocæans,**
One State entire, accursing the return;—
  Go *we* wherever a free foot may lead us,
No matter what the billow or the blast,
  Welcome alike be Africus or Notus.
Are ye agreed?† Who can this vote amend?
  Why pause? To sea! accept the favouring auspice.
Yet ere we part thus swear: When the firm rocks,
  In the deep bosom of the ocean buried, §
Rise to the light and float along the wave,
  Then, nor till then, return for us be lawful!
Back unrepentant we will veer the sail
  When Po shall lave the summits of Matinus;
When into ocean just the Apennine;
  When herds no longer fear the tawny lions;

---

* "Quæque carent ventis et solibus ossa Quirini." I have rendered the simple meaning of the line, but the literal construction is, that he shall scatter the bones of Romulus, hitherto free, in their secret place, from wind and sun. Elsewhere (Car. III. 3, 16) Horace speaks of Romulus as rapt to heaven, according to the popular belief. Varro, according to Porphyrion, says the tomb of Romulus was behind the Rostra. Orelli suggests that Romulus

Barbarus, heu! cineres insistet victor, et Urbem
    Eques sonante verberabit ungula,
Quæque carent ventis et solibus ossa Quirini, *
    Nefas videre! dissipabit insolens.
Forte quid expediat communiter aut melior pars
    Malis carere quæritis laboribus;
Nulla sit hac potior sententia: Phocæorum
    Velut profugit exsecrata civitas**
Agros atque Lares patrios, habitandaque fana
    Apris reliquit et rapacibus lupis;
Ire pedes quocunque ferent, quocunque per undas
    Notus vocabit, aut protervus Africus.
Sic placet? † an melius quis habet suadere?   Secunda
    Ratem occupare quid moramur alite?
Sed juremus in hæc:—Simul imis saxa renarint
    Vadis levata, ne redire sit nefas;
Neu conversa domum pigeat dare lintea, quando
    Padus Matina laverit cacumina,
In mare seu celsus procurrerit Appenninus,
    Novaque monstra junxerit libidine

---

*(Quirinus) is not literally signified in the verse, but rather symbolically, as the ideal representative (*der ideale repræsentant*) of the other Roman citizens, whose bones shall be scattered to wind and sun.

** "Phocæorum—exsecrata civitas." "Exsecrata" is used in a double sense, "binding themselves under a curse."—MACLEANE. The oath of the Phocæans, who left their city when besieged by Harpagus (Herod. I. 165) never to return till an iron bar they threw into the sea should float on the surface, is amplified in the oath which Horace suggests to his political friends.

† "Sic placet"—"placetne," the usual formula. The poet fancies himself addressing a meeting of the citizens.—MACLEANE.

§ "In the deep bosom of the ocean buried."—SHAKESPEARE.

When nature's self becomes unnatural,
  And, love reversing all its old conditions,
Tigers woo does, the kite pairs with the dove;
  When into scales the he-goat smooths his fleeces,
And quits the hill-top for the briny seas.
  So swear, swear aught that cuts us off for ever
From the old homes, and go, one State entire,
  Accursing the return. If all not willing,
At least that part which is of nobler mind
  Than the unteachable herd. To beds ill-omened
Let those nought hoping, those nought daring, cling.
  Ye in whom manhood lives, cease woman wailings,
Wing the sail far beyond Etruscan shores.
  Lo! where awaits an all-circumfluent ocean—
Fields, the Blest Fields we seek, the Golden Isles
  Where teems a land that never knows the plough-
      share—
Where, never needing pruner, laughs the vine—
  Where the dusk fig adorns the stem it springs from,*
And the glad olive ne'er its pledge belies **—
  There from the creviced ilex wells the honey;
There, down the hillside bounding light, the rills
  Dance with free foot, whose fall is heard in music;
There, without call, the she-goat yields her milk,
  And back to browse, with unexhausted udders,
Wanders the friendly flock; no hungry bear
  Growls round the sheepfold in the starry gloaming,†
Nor high with rippling vipers heaves the soil. §
  These, and yet more of marvel, shall we witness,

---

  * Viz., ungrafted.
  ** "Nunquam fallentis termes olivæ." The olive crop is still
as fickle as the English hop crop—one good year for two bad ones

Mirus amor, juvet ut tigres subsidere cervis,
    Adulteretur et columba miluo,
Credula nec ravos timeant armenta leones,
    Ametque salsa levis hircus æquora.—
Hæc, et quæ poterunt reditus abscindere dulces,
    Eamus omnis exsecrata civitas,
Aut pars indocili melior grege; mollis et exspes
    Inominata perprimat cubilia!
Vos, quibus est virtus, muliebrem tollite luctum,
    Etrusca præter et volate litora.
Nos manet Oceanus circumvagus: arva, beata
    Petamus arva divites et insulas;
Reddit ubi Cererem tellus inarata quotannis,
    Et imputata floret usque vinea,
Germinat et nunquam fallentis termes olivæ,**
    Suamque pulla ficus ornat arborem,
Mella cava manant ex ilice, montibus altis
    Levis crepante lympha desilit pede.
Illic injussæ veniunt ad mulctra capellæ,
    Refertque tenta grex amicus ubera;
Nec vespertinus circumgemit ursus ovile, †
    Neque intumescit alta viperis humus. §

---

is the accredited average. The olive crop, like the hop, was and still is often ruinous, from the speculative gambling which its uncertainty tends to stimulate. Horace says that which came home to every olive-grower when he speaks of an olive-tree that never deceived its cultivator.

    † "Vespertinus ursus."

    § "Neque intumescit alta viperis humus." Orelli, in one of those notes, exquisite for accuracy of perception, in which his edition is so rich, objects to the common translation of "alta humus"—mountainous or rising ground, in which vipers are not found. He suggests, on various Greek authorities, that "alta," in

We, for felicity reserved; how ne'er
　Dank Eurus sweeps the fields with flooding rain-storm,
Nor rich seeds parch within the sweltering glebe.
　Either extreme the King of Heaven has tempered.
Thither ne'er rowed the oar of Argonaut,
　The impure Colchian never there had footing.
There Sidon's trader brought no lust of gain;
　No weary toil there anchored with Ulysses;
Sickness is known not; on the tender lamb
　No ray falls baneful from one star in heaven.
When Jove's decree alloyed the golden age,
　He kept these shores for one pure race secreted;
For all beside the golden age grew brass
　Till the last centuries hardened to the iron,
Whence to the pure in heart a glad escape,†
　By favour of my prophet-strain is given. §

its sense of "deep," not "high," has the signification of "fertile" (we say a deep rich soil, in antithesis to a thin poor one); and to those who dissent from that interpretation, Orelli commends Jahn's proposed construction to take "alta" with "intumescit"—"swells high." Macleane indorses it. Orelli refers "tumescit" not to the sweltering venom, but to the undulous movement of the reptile, alternately rising and falling, so that the ground literally seems to heave, as the commentator in Orelli says he has himself noticed, in his solitary walks along the meadows and water-banks of Italy, which, but for the vipers, would have been exceedingly pleasant. In the translation it is sought to render this idea, drawn from the critic's personal observation, and which, as a friend suggests, is in curious accordance with a passage in Humboldt's 'Aspects of Nature,' where he describes the reptiles, snakes, breaking their way through the clay soil left by the inundations of the Orinoco, and lifting the ground into little heaps. Ritter finds fault with Orelli's interpretation, and contends that "alta" denotes the high grass and herbage of the soil.

* "Aquosus Eurus arva radat imbribus." The literal and vernacular meaning of "rado" is "to shave," as "radere caput;"

EPODE XVI.

Pluraque felices mirabimur: ut neque largis
    Aquosus Eurus arva radat imbribus,*
Pinguia nec siccis urantur semina glebis;
    Utrumque rege temperante cælitum.
Non huc Argoo contendit remige pinus,
    Neque impudica Colchis intulit pedem;
Non huc Sidonii torserunt cornua nautæ,
    Laboriosa nec cohors Ulixëi.
Nulla nocent pecori contagia, nullius astri
    Gregem æstuosa torret impotentia.
Jupiter illa piæ secrevit litora genti,
    Ut inquinavit ære tempus aureum;
Ære, dehinc ferro duravit sæcula; quorum †
    Piis secunda, vate me, datur fuga.

---

* "radere littora" (generally construed "to coast along") is better interpreted by the phrase familiar enough to our English sailor, "to shave the shore." Orelli here construes "radat" "deluges," or "lays waste."

† "Quorum" depends on "fuga"—flight from the iron ages. "Piis" has the signification of "pure from crime."

§ It has been supposed by some that the description of these happy islands, and the idea of migrating thither, is taken from the account of the Western Islands, which almost tempted Sertorius to seek in them a refuge from the cares of his life, and the harassment of unceasing wars. This story, which is told by Plutarch in his life of Sertorius, is said by Acron to have been given by Sallust. But the general tradition of a happy land separated from the rest of the world was popular among the ancients from the earliest time, and Horace might have got the notion from Hesiod or Pindar. The poem, however, would assume a much deeper and more earnest character if we could suppose that the passage in question has a symbolical signification, and refers to the isle of happy souls in which Achilles was wed to Helen. In that case the latent meaning would apply to another world beyond this, and its moral would be, "Rather than submit to the ills and ignominy in store for us, let us take our chance of those seats in Elysium reserved for the pure."

EPODE XVII.

TO CANIDIA—IN APOLOGY.

This poem completes Horace's attacks on Canidia by an ironical pretence of submission and apology. I state in a note my conjecture that he was really suffering

Now, O now, I submit to the might of thy science;
    Now behold, as a suppliant, I lift up my hands!
I adjure thee by Proserpine, and by great Hecate—
    I adjure thee by all the most pitiless Powers—
I adjure thee by all thy weird black-books of magic,
    Strong in charms to call down loosened stars from the sky—
Dread Canidia, O spare me thy grim incantations!
    And O slacken, O slacken, thy swift-whirling wheel!*
Even Telephus moved the fierce grandson of Nereus,†
    Against whom he had marshalled, in insolent pride,
The host of his Mysians, and levelled his arrows;—
    Even Hector the homicide (sternly consigned
To the maw of the dog and the beak of the vulture)
    Weeping matrons of Troy were allowed to embalm,
After Priam, alas (his stout walls left behind him)
    At the feet of the stubborn Achilles knelt down.

---

* "Citumque retro solve, solve turbinem." All the MSS. have "solve." Lambinus has "volve" without authority. "Turbo" is a wheel of some sort used by sorceresses; "rhombos" is the Greek name for it. Ovid, Propertius, and Martial mention it.—MACLEANE. This critic considers that "retro solvere" means to relax the onward motion of the wheel, which will then of itself roll back. I may observe that "turbo," which means both a whirlwind and a spinning-top, probably implies the shape of the witch's wheel, as

fering from an illness when it was written. There is no reason to infer with some, that, because he says his hair was turning grey, the verses were written in later life. "But now at thirty years my hair is grey," says Byron. At what age Horace detected his first grey hair—and he became grey early—no one can guess. The poem has all the character of the early ones comprised in this book. It is the only epode in which the same metre (trimeter iambic) is adopted.

CARM. XVII.

Jam jam efficaci do manus scientiæ,
Supplex, et oro regna per Proserpinæ,
Per et Dianæ non movenda numina,
Per atque libros carminum valentium
Refixa cælo devocare sidera,
Canidia, parce vocibus tandem sacris,
Citumque retro solve, solve turbinem.*
Movit nepotem Telephus Nereïum,†
In quem superbus ordinarat agmina
Mysorum, et in quem tela acuta torserat.
Unxere matres Iliæ addictum feris
Alitibus atque canibus homicidam Hectorem,
Postquam relictis mœnibus rex procidit
Heu! pervicacis ad pedes Achilleï.

being wide at its upper part (the hoop), and spiral at the bottom. Party-coloured threads attached to it formed a web to entangle the victim operated upon.

† Telephus, king of Mysia, opposed the Greeks on their expedition to Troy, was wounded by Achilles, grandson of Nereus, and son of Thetis. Achilles cured him by the scrapings of the spear with which he was wounded.

So the rowers of toil-worn Ulysses, with Circe
    Released from the force of enchantment, at will,
Giving back to limbs bristled* the voice and the reason,
    And the glory that dwells in the aspect of Man.
Enough, and much more than enough, for all penance
    Thy wrath has inflicted, O greatly beloved—
O greatly beloved both by huckster and sailor!**
    Fled away from my form is the vigour of youth,
And the blush-rose of health from my cheeks has departed,
    Leaving nought but pale bones scantly covered with skin.
And my hair is grown grey with the spell of thy perfumes;
    From my suffering I snatch not a moment's repose.
Still the night vexes day, and still day the night vexes;
    I can free not the lungs strained with gaspings for
        breath.†
Wherefore, wretch that I am, I confess myself conquered;
    I acknowledge the truth I had dared to deny;
Yes, the chant of a Samnite can rattle a bosom,
    And the Marsian's witch-ditty can split up a head!
What more wouldst thou have? Earth and Sea! I am hotter
    Than Alcides in fell Nessian venom imbued,
Or than Sicily's flame budding fresh in fierce Ætna.§
    Dost thou mean, then, for ever to keep up this fire—

---

  * Previously transformed to swine. Bentley's reading of Circa instead of Circe (the Latin instead of the Greek termination), founded on the statement of Valerius Probus, is adopted by all the more recent editors.

  ** As the lowest of the low.

† "Neque est
Levare tenta spiritu præcordia."

The symptoms described are those of a real malady—emaciation, fever, sleeplessness, difficulty of breathing—a malady familiar enough to those who have experienced an Italian malaria. The

Setosa duris exuere pellibus
Laboriosi remiges Ulixeī,
Volente Circa, membra;* tunc mens et sonus
Relapsus, atque notus in voltus honor.
Dedi satis superque pœnarum tibi,
Amata nautis multum et institoribus.**
Fugit juventas, et verecundus color
Reliquit ossa pelle amicta lurida;
Tuis capillus albus est odoribus;
Nullum ab labore me reclinat otium;
Urget diem nox, et dies noctem, neque est
Levare tenta spiritu præcordia.†
Ergo negatum vincor ut credam miser,
Sabella pectus increpare carmina,
Caputque Marsa dissilire nenia.
Quid amplius vis? O mare, O terra! ardeo,
Quantum neque atro delibutus Hercules
Nessi cruore, nec Sicana fervida
Virens in Ætna flamma;§ tu, donec cinis
Injuriosis aridus ventis ferar,

whole poem seems to me to have the air of being written at some period of actual illness, in the attempt to draw amusement from humorous exaggeration of his own complaints, which is common enough among witty invalids. The nature of the poem would perhaps scarcely suggest itself to him if he were quite well in health at the time.

§ "Nec Sicana fervida
Virens in Ætna flamma."

I take "virens" to have the same signification here that it has Lib. IV. Carm. xiii. 6, "Virentis doctæ psallere Chiæ"—*i.e.*, youthful, blooming or budding, in the spring of life. "Virens flamma" may be compared with Lucretius's "Flos flammæ." I agree, therefore, with Macleane, who follows Lambinus and the scholiast in Cruquius, in interpreting the meaning to be "the flame,

O thou warehouse of venomous fuel from Colchis,—
   Till I'm whirled, a parched cinder, the waif of the winds?
What the death that awaits or the fine that redeems me?
   Every penalty asked I will honestly pay:
Speak! a hundred young steers; or a couple of stanzas
   To be sung to a lute-string attuned to a lie,
I will chant thee as chaste, I will chant thee as honest;
   Thou shalt traverse, a gold constellation, the stars.
Moved by prayer Castor's self, and the twin of great Castor,
   Gave back sight to the bard who had Helen defamed.*
So mayst thou, for thou canst, from this frenzy release me—
   O thou, by no filth-scum paternal defiled **—
O thou who didst never, an agéd wise-woman, †
   From his grave the first day § rake a beggar-man's dust!

always fresh and renewing itself," and having no more to do with the colour of the flame as of sulphurous green, which is the supposition favoured by Orelli and Dillenburger, than it has in the line quoted above, where it is certainly not meant to imply that Chia is "green." The emendation of "furens," suggested by Bentley on inferior MS. authority, and rejected by most recent commentators, would substitute a prosaic commonplace for a poetic image.

* "Infamis Helenæ Castor offensus vicem,
   Fraterque magni Castoris, victi prece."

The poet alluded to is Stesichorus, punished with blindness for libelling Helen, and recovering his sight after writing an apology (palinodia), of which a fragment remains. Other writers ascribe to Helen the grace of restoring the poet's sight. Probably Horace follows some other version of the story lost to us, in attributing the restoration to her two brothers. The allusion to Castor and Pollux, twin stars, comes naturally enough after saying that Canidia shall become a constellation herself.

** "Obsoleta." This word, as Macleane observes, is applied in an unusual sense. It usually signifies "that which is gone to decay," "out of use;" and so it comes to mean that which is spoilt and worthless (in which sense Macleane implies that he would take

Cales venenis officina Colchicis.
Quæ finis, aut quod me manet stipendium?
Effare; jussas cum fide pœnas luam,
Paratus expiare, seu poposceris
Centum juvencos, sive mendaci lyra
Voles sonari: tu pudica, tu proba
Perambulabis astra sidus aureum.
Infamis Helenæ Castor offensus vicem,
Fraterque magni Castoris, victi prece,*
Adempta vati reddidere lumina.
Et tu, potes nam, solve me dementia,
O nec paternis obsoleta** sordibus,
Neque in sepulcris pauperum prudens anus †
Novendiales dissipare pulveres. §

it here). Orelli, I think, better explains it as "inquinata," "deformata." I apprehend that "inquinata," in the sense of "stained," or "defiled," is the right meaning—as in Seneca (Agam. 971, a line which appears to have escaped the commentators on the passage), "Dextera obsoleta sanguine."

† "Neque in sepulcris pauperum prudens anus." Macleane, in his note on Canidia, Epode III. p. 280, observes, that Horace says Canidia is not an old woman, and refers to this very line as proving it. It proves just the contrary. Horace, speaking in the most obvious irony, had before asked if he should celebrate her with a lying lyre, and all he is now saying about her is, of course, to be read in the opposite sense.

§ "Novendiales pulveres." This has been variously interpreted; but Orelli and all recent commentators agree in accepting the general authority of Servius, Ad. Æn. 5, that the ashes were buried the ninth day after death—the body having been burned on the eighth. Probably enough the poor were not kept so long above ground; but the phrase "novendiales" might have come into conventional usage as signifying the first day of burial. It means, at all events, fresh buried, while warmth was yet in the ashes—that being essential for the purposes of witchcraft; and the ashes were scattered and reduced to powder for those purposes.

O thy breast is the kindest, thy hands are the purest
  On earth; Pactumeius is really thy son;*
And whenever thou bearest the pangs of a mother,
  'Tis to rise from thy bed with the bloom of a maid!

CANIDIA'S REPLY.

"Why on ears locked against thee pour prayer unavailing?
  Not more deaf to the sailor, stripped bare to the skin,
Are the rocks upon which, in the depth of the winter,
  Breaks in thunder the reef of a merciless sea.
What, forsooth! raise a laugh at the rites of Cotytto †
  Divulged? Mock the Cupid of Cupids most free?
As if thou wert high-priest to the witchcraft of charnels,
  And in safety mightst make a town-talk of my name!
What my gain to have squandered on beldames Pelignian
  My gold, and have mixed up the poisons most quick?
Yet they are not so quick, but their work shall seem tardy §
  To thy longings for death to escape from thy pain.
Ay, for this shall thy thankless existence be lengthened,
  That with every new day there shall come a new pang.
For reprieve sighed the father of Pelops the faithless,
  Hungry Tantalus, yearning in vain for the food;
For reprieve sighed Prometheus, fast bound to the vulture,
  And Sisyphus upward vain-heaving the stone.

---

* "Tuusque venter Pactumeius." It would seem that the person, whoever she might have been, represented by Canidia, was rather sensitive to the charge of sterility, or that, for some reason or other, she had palmed off a supposititious child (Pactumeius) as her own. In the former poem on Canidia, Horace had implied a doubt if she had any real offspring, "Si vocata partubus Lucina veris affuit." He now ironically appears to make it up with her,

EPODE XVII.

Tibi hospitale pectus et puræ manus,
Tuusque venter Pactumeius,* et tuo
Cruore rubros obstetrix pannos lavit,
Utcunque fortis exilis puerpera.

CANIDIA.

'Quid obseratis auribus fundis preces?
Non saxa nudis surdiora navitis
Neptunus alto tundit hibernus salo.
Inultus ut tu riseris Cotyttia †
Vulgata, sacrum liberi Cupidinis,
Et Esquilini Pontifex venefici
Impune ut Urbem nomine impleris meo?
Quid proderat ditasse Pelignas anus,
Velociusve miscuisse toxicum?
Sed tardiora fata te votis manent: §
Ingrata misero vita ducenda est in hoc,
Novis ut usque suppetas laboribus.
Optat quietem Pelopis infidi pater,
Egens benignæ Tantalus semper dapis;
Optat Prometheus obligatus aliti;
Optat supremo collocare Sisyphus
In monte saxum; sed vetant leges Jovis.
Voles modo altis desilire turribus,

---

by declaring that Pactumeius is really her son. Ritter has partumeius instead of Pactumeius.

† The rites of Cotytto, of Thracian origin, were celebrated only by women, with one presiding priest.

§ "Sed tardiora fata te votis manent." There is dispute about the reading and interpretation of this passage. I adopt those sanctioned by Orelli and Macleane.

But reprieve is just that which Jove's law has denied thee.
  So shalt thou, in the weary revolt from thy woes,
Now wish to leap down from the height of a turret,
  Now with Norican blade to gash open thy breast,
And to garland thy throat with a noose, but wish vainly.
  Conquered foe, on thy shoulders in state I will ride,
And the earth shall acknowledge my scorn and my
    triumph.
What! shall I who, as thou, curious fool, knowest well,
Mould and move human life in the wax of an image;
  Who can snatch with my chantings the moon from
    the sky;
Who can raise up the dead, though consumed into ashes,
  And can temper at pleasure the bowl of desire;—
What! shall I bring mine arts to an end in lamenting
  That they have not the slightest effect upon thee?"

Modo ense pectus Norico recludere,
Frustraque vincla gutturi nectes tuo,
Fastidiosa tristis ægrimonia.
Vectabor humeris tunc ego inimicis eques,
Meæque terra cedet insolentiæ.
An quæ movere cereas imagines,
Ut ipse nosti curiosus, et polo
Deripere lunam vocibus possim meis,
Possim crematos excitare mortuos,
Desiderique temperare pocula,
Plorem artis, in te nil agentis, exitus?'

THE END.

PRINTING OFFICE OF THE PUBLISHER.

www.ingramcontent.com/pod-product-compliance
Lightning Source LLC
Chambersburg PA
CBHW032042230426
43672CB00009B/1435